Rhymes of a Rolling Stone

Rhymes of a Rolling Stone

BY

ROBERT W. SERVICE

Author of
"Songs of a Sourdough," "Ballads of a Cheechako,"
"The Trail of '98"

McGraw-Hill Ryerson Limited

Toronto   Montreal   New York   London   Sydney
Johannesburg   Mexico   Panama   Düsseldorf
Singapore   Rio de Janeiro   Kuala Lumpur   New Delhi

ISBN 0-07-077715-2

1 2 3 4 5 6 7 8 9 HR 5 4 3 2 1 0 9 8 7

PRINTED AND BOUND IN CANADA

I have no doubt at all the Devil grins
    As seas of ink I spatter;
Ye gods, forgive my "literary" sins—
    The other kind don't matter.

PRELUDE

I sing no idle songs of dalliance days,
  No dreams Elysian inspire my rhyming;
I have no Celia to enchant my lays,
  No pipes of Pan have set my heart to chiming.
I am no wordsmith dripping gems divine
  Into the golden chalice of a sonnet;
If love songs witch you, close this book of mine,
    Waste no time on it.

Yet bring I to my work an eager joy,
  A lusty love of life and all things human;
Still in me leaps the wonder of the boy,
  A pride in man, a deathless faith in woman.
Still red blood calls, still rings the valiant fray;
  Adventure beacons through the summer
    gloaming:
Oh, long and long and long will be the day
    Ere I come homing!

PRELUDE

This earth is ours to love: lute, brush and pen,
  They are but tongues to tell of life sincerely;
The thaumaturgic Day, the might of men,
  O God of Scribes, grant us to grave them
      clearly!
Grant heart that homes in heart, then all is well.
  Honey is honey-sweet, howe'er the hiving.
Each to his work, his wage at evening bell
      The strength of striving.

CONTENTS

———

CONTENTS

CONTENTS

13

CONTENTS

14

CONTENTS

15

CONTENTS

16

A ROLLING STONE

There's sunshine in the heart of me,
  My blood sings in the breeze;
The mountains are a part of me,
  I'm fellow to the trees.
My golden youth I'm squandering,
  Sun-libertine am I;
A-wandering, a-wandering,
  Until the day I die.

I was once, I declare, a Stone Age man,
  And I roomed in the cool of a cave;
I have known, I will swear, in a new life-**span,**
  The fret and the sweat of a slave:
For far over all that folks hold **worth,**
  There lives and there leaps in me
A love of the lowly things of earth,
  And a passion to be free.

17

A ROLLING STONE

To pitch my tent with no prosy plan,
   To range and to change at will;
To mock at the mastership of man,
   To seek Adventure's thrill.
Carefree to be, as a bird that sings,
   To go my own sweet way;
To reck not at all what may befall,
   But to live and to love each day.

To make my body a temple pure
   Wherein I dwell serene;
To care for the things that shall endure,
   The simple, sweet and clean.
To oust out envy and hate and rage,
   To breathe with no alarm;
For Nature shall be my anchorage,
   And none shall do me harm.

To shun all lures that debauch the soul,
   The orgied rites of the rich;
To eat my crust as a rover must
   With the rough-neck down in the ditch
To trudge by his side whate'er betide;
   To share his fire at night;
To call him friend to the long trail-end,
   And to read his heart aright.

A ROLLING STONE

To scorn all strife, and to view all life
  With the curious eyes of a child;
From the plangent sea to the prairie,
  From the slum to the heart of the Wild.
From the red-rimmed star to the speck of sand,
  From the vast to the greatly small;
For I know that the whole for good is planned,
  And I want to see it all.

To see it all, the wide world-way,
  From the fig-leaf belt to the Pole;
With never a one to say me nay,
  And none to cramp my soul.
In belly-pinch I will pay the price,
  But God! let me be free;
For once I know in the long ago,
  They made a slave of me.

In a flannel shirt from earth's clean dirt,
  Here, pal, is my calloused hand!
  Oh, I love each day as a rover may,
  Nor seek to understand.
To *enjoy* is good enough for me;
  The gipsy of God am I;

A ROLLING STONE

Then here's a hail to each flaring dawn!
And here's a cheer to the night that's gone!
And may I go a-roaming on
  Until the day I die!

Then every star shall sing to me
  Its song of liberty;
And every morn shall bring to me
  Its mandate to be free.
In every throbbing vein of me
  I'll feel the vast Earth-call:
O body, heart and brain of me,
  Praise Him who made it all!

THE SOLDIER OF FORTUNE

"DENY your God!" they ringed me with their
  spears;
  Blood-crazed were they, and reeking from the
    strife;
Hell-hot their hate, and venom-fanged their
  sneers,
  And one man spat on me and nursed a knife.
And there was I, sore wounded and alone,
  I, the last living of my slaughtered band.
Oh, sinister the sky, and cold as stone!
  In one red laugh of horror reeled the land.
And dazed and desperate I faced their spears,
  And like a flame out-leaped that naked knife,
And like a serpent stung their bitter jeers:
  "Deny your God, and we will give you life."

Deny my God! Oh, life was very sweet!
  And it is hard in youth and hope to die;
And there my comrades dear lay at my feet,
  And in that blear of blood soon must I lie.

THE SOLDIER OF FORTUNE

And yet . . . I almost laughed—it seemed
    so odd,
  For long and long had I not vainly tried
To reason out and body forth my God,
    And prayed for light, and doubted—and
      denied.
Denied the Being I could not conceive,
  Denied a life-to-be beyond the grave. . . .
And now they ask me, who do not believe,
  Just to deny, to voice my doubt, to save
This life of mine that sings so in the sun,
  The bloom of youth yet red upon my cheek,
My only life!—O fools! 'tis easy done,
  I will deny . . . and yet I do not speak.

" Deny your God!" their spears are all agleam,
  And I can see their eyes with blood-lust shine;
Their snarling voices shrill into a scream,
  And, mad to slay, they quiver for the sign.
Deny my God! yes, I could do it well;
  Yet if I did, what of my race, my name?
How they would spit on me, these dogs of hell!
  Spurn me, and put on me the brand of shame.
A white man's honour! what of that, I say?
  Shall these black curs cry " Coward " in my
    face?

THE SOLDIER OF FORTUNE

They who would perish for their gods of clay—
   Shall I defile my country and my race?
My country! what's my country to me now?
   Soldier of Fortune, free and far I roam;
All men are brothers in my heart, I vow;
   The wide and wondrous world is all my home.
My country! reverent of her splendid Dead,
   Her heroes proud, her martyrs pierced with
        pain:
For me her puissant blood was vainly shed;
   For me her drums of battle beat in vain,
And free I fare, half-heedless of her fate:
   No faith, no flag, I owe—then why not seek
This last loop-hole of life? Why hesitate?
   I will deny . . . and yet I do not speak.

"Deny your God!" their spears are poised on
       high,
   And tense and terrible they wait the word;
And dark and darker glooms the dreary sky,
   And in that hush of horror no thing stirred.
Then, through the ringing terror and sheer hate
   Leaped there a vision to me—Oh, how far!
A face, Her face . . . through all my stormy
       fate
   A joy, a strength, a glory and a star.

THE SOLDIER OF FORTUNE

Beneath the pines, where lonely camp-fires
    gleam,
  In seas forlorn, amid the deserts drear,
How I had gladdened to that face of dream!
  And never, never had it seemed so dear.
O silken hair that veils the sunny brow!
  O eyes of grey, so tender and so true!
O lips of smiling sweetness! must I now
  Forever and forever go from you?
Ah, yes, I must . . . for if I do this thing,
  How can I look into your face again?
Knowing you think me more than half a king,
  I with my craven heart, my honour slain.
No! no! my mind's made up. I gaze above,
  Into that sky insensate as a stone;
Not for my creed, my country, but my Love
  Will I stand up and meet my death alone.
Then, though it be to utter dark I sink,
  The God that dwells in me is not denied;
" Best " triumphs over " Beast "—and so I think
  Humanity itself is glorified. . . .

" And now, my butchers, I embrace my fate.
  Come! let my heart's blood slake the thirsty
    sod.
Curst be the life you offer! Glut your hate!
  Strike! Strike, you dogs! I'll *not* deny my
    God."

THE SOLDIER OF FORTUNE

I saw the spears that seemed a-leap to slay,
   All quiver earthward at the headman's nod;
And in a daze of dream I heard him say:
   " Go, set him free who serves so well his God!"

THE GRAMOPHONE AT FOND-DU-LAC

Now Eddie Malone got a swell grammyfone, to
    draw all the trade to his store;
An' sez he: " Come along for a season of song,
    which the like ye had niver before."
Then Dogrib an' Slave, an' Yellow-knife brave,
    an' Cree in his dinky canoe,
Confluated near, to see an' to hear Ed's grammy-
    fone make its dayboo.

Then Ed turned the crank, an' there on the bank
    they squatted like bumps on a log.
For acres around there wasn't a sound, not even
    the howl of a dog.
When out of the horn there sudden was born
    such a marvellous elegant tone;
An' then like a spell on that auddyence fell the
    voice of its first grammyfone.

THE GRAMOPHONE AT FOND-DU-LAC

" *Bad medicine!*" cried Old Tom, the One-eyed,
      an' made for to jump in the lake;
But no one gave heed to his little stampede, so
      he guessed he had made a mistake.
Then Roll-in-the-Mud, a chief of the blood,
      observed in choice Chippewayan:
" You've brought us canned beef, an' it's now
      my belief, that this here's a case of
      ' *canned man.*' "

Well, though I'm not strong on the Dago in
      song, that sure got me goin' for fair.
There was Crusoe an' Scotty an' Ma'am Shoe-
      man Hank, an' Melber an' Bonchy was
      there.
'Twas silver an' gold, an' sweetness untold, to
      hear all them big guinneys sing;
An' thick all around an' inhalin' the sound, them
      Indians formed in a ring.

So solemn they sat, an' they smoked an' they
      spat, but their eyes sort o' glistened an'
      shone;
Yet niver a word of approvin' occurred till that
      guy Harry Lauder came on.

THE GRAMOPHONE AT FOND-DU-LAC

Then hunter of moose an' squaw an' papoose
    jest laughed till their stummicks was
    sore;
Six times Eddie set back that record an' yet
    they hollered an' hollered for more.

I'll never forget that frame-up, you bet; them
    caverns of sunset agleam;
Them still peaks aglow, them shadders below,
    an' the lake like a petrified dream;
The teepees that stood by the edge of the wood;
    the evenin' star blinkin' alone;
The peace an' the rest, an' final an' best, the
    music of Ed's grammyfone.

Then sudden an' clear there rang on my ear a
    song mighty simple an' old;
Heart-hungry an' high it thrilled to the sky, all
    about " silver threads in the gold."
'Twas tender to tears, an' it brung back the
    years, the mem'ries that hallow an' yearn;
'Twas home-love an' joy, 'twas the thought of
    my boy .   .   . an' right there I vowed
    I'd return.

THE GRAMOPHONE AT FOND-DU-LAC

Big Four-finger Jack was right at my back, **an'**
    I saw with a kind o' surprise,
He gazed at the lake with a heartful of ache,
    an' the tears irrigated his eyes.
An' sez he: " Cuss me, pard! but that there hits
    me hard; I've a mother does nuthin' but
    wait.
" She's turned eighty-three, an' she's only got
    me, an' I'm scared it'll soon be too late."

    *   *   *   *   *

On Fond-du-lac's shore I'm hearin' once more
    that blessed old grammyfone play.
The summer's all gone, an' I'm still livin' **on in**
    the same old haphazardous way.
Oh, I cut out the booze, an' with muscles an'
    thews I corralled all the coin to go back;
But it wasn't to be—he'd a mother, you see—
    so I—*slipped it to Four-finger Jack.*

THE LAND OF BEYOND

HAVE ever you heard of the Land of Beyond,
　That dreams at the gates of the day?
Alluring it lies at the skirts of the skies,
　And ever so far away;
Alluring it calls: O ye the yoke galls,
　And ye of the trail overfond,
With saddle and pack, by paddle and track,
　Let's go to the Land of Beyond!

Have ever you stood where the silences brood,
　And vast the horizons begin,
At the dawn of the day to behold far away
　The goal you would strive for and win?
Yet, ah! in the night when you gain to the
　　　height,
　With the vast pool of heaven star-spawned,
Afar and agleam, like a valley of dream,
　Still mocks you a Land of Beyond.

30

THE LAND OF BEYOND

Thank God! there is always a Land of Beyond
  For us who are true to the trail;
A vision to seek, a beckoning peak,
  A farness that never will fail;
A pride in our soul that mocks at a goal,
  A manhood that irks at a bond,
And try how we will, unattainable still,
  Behold it, our Land of Beyond!

SUNSHINE

I.

FLAT as a drum-head stretch the haggard
      snows;
  The mighty skies are palisades of light;
The stars are blurred; the silence grows and
      grows;
  Vaster and vaster vaults the icy night.
Here in my sleeping-bag I cower and pray:
" Silence and night, have pity; stoop and slay."

I have not slept for many, many days.
  I close my eyes with weariness—that's all.
I still have strength to feed the drift-wood blaze
  That flickers weirdly on the icy wall.
I still have strength to pray: " God rest her
      soul,
  Here in the awful shadow of the Pole."

SUNSHINE

There in the cabin's alcove low she lies,
   Still candles gleaming at her head and feet;
All snow-drop white, ash-cold, with closèd eyes,
   Lips smiling, hands at rest—O God, how
         sweet!
How all unutterably sweet she seems . . .
Not dead, not dead, indeed—she dreams, she
         dreams.

II

" Sunshine," I called her, and she brought,
         I vow,
   God's blessed sunshine to this life of mine.
I was a rover, of the breed who plough
   Life's furrow in a far-flung, lonely line;
The wilderness my home, my fortune cast
In a wild land of dearth, barbaric, vast.

When did I see her first? Long had I lain
   Groping my way to life through fevered
         gloom.
Sudden the cloud of darkness left my brain;
   A velvet bar of sunshine pierced the room,
And in that mellow glory aureoled
She stood, she stood, all golden in its gold.

SUNSHINE

Sunshine! O miracle! the earth grew glad;
　Radiant each blade of grass, each living
　　　thing.
What a huge strength, high hope, proud will I
　　　had!
　All the wide world with rapture seemed to
　　　ring.
Would she but wed me?　*Yes:* then fared we
　　　forth
Into the vast, unvintageable North.

III.

In Muskrat Land the conies leap,
　The wavies linger in their flight;
The jewelled, snake-like rivers creep;
　The sun, sad rogue, is out all night;
The great wood-bison paws the sand,
In Muskrat Land, in Muskrat Land.

In Muskrat Land dim streams divide
　The tundras belted by the sky.
How sweet in slim canoe to glide,
　And dream, and let the world go by!
Build gay camp-fires on greening strand!
In Muskrat Land, in Muskrat Land.

SUNSHINE

IV.

And so we dreamed and drifted, she and I;
   And how she loved that free, unfathomed
      life!
There, in the peach-bloom of the midnight sky,
   The silence welded us, true man and wife.
Then North and North invincibly we pressed
Beyond the Circle, to the world's white crest.

And on the wind-flailed Arctic waste we stayed
   Dwelt with the Huskies by the Polar sea.
Fur had they, white fox, marten, mink, to trade,
   And we had food-stuff, bacon, flour and tea.
So we made snug, chummed up with all the
      band:
Sudden the Winter swooped on Husky Land.

V.

What was that ill so sinister and dread,
   Smiting the tribe with sickness to the bone?
So that we waked one morn to find them fled;
   So that we stood and stared, alone, alone.

SUNSHINE

Bravely she smiled and looked into my eyes;
  Laughed at their troubled, stern, foreboding
      pain;
Gaily she mocked the menace of the skies,
  Turned to our cheery cabin once again,
Saying: " 'Twill soon be over, dearest one,
The long, long night: then O the sun, the sun!"

VI.

God made a heart of gold, of gold,
  Shining and sweet and true;
Gave it a home of fairest mould.
  Blest it, and called it—You.

God gave the rose its grace of glow,
  And the lark its radiant glee;
But, better than all, I know, I know
  God gave you, Heart, to me.

VII.

She was all sunshine in those dubious days;
  Our cabin beaconed with defiant light;
We chattered by the friendly drift-wood blaze;
  Closer and closer cowered the hag-like night.

SUNSHINE

A wolf-howl would have been a welcome sound,
  And there was none in all that stricken land;
Yet with such silence, darkness, death around,
  Learned we to love as few can understand.
Spirit with spirit fused, and soul to soul,
There in the sullen shadow of the Pole.

VIII.

What was that haunting horror of the night?
  Brave was she; buoyant, full of sunny cheer.
Why was her face so small, so strangely white?
  Then did I turn from her, heart-sick with
          fear;
Sought in my agony the outcast snows;
  Prayed in my pain to that insensate sky;
Grovelled and sobbed and cursed, and then
          arose:
  "Sunshine! O heart of gold! to die! to die!"

IX.

She died on Christmas Day—it seems so sad
  That one you love should die on Christmas
          Day.
Head-bowed I knelt by her; O God! I had
  No tears to shed, no moan, no prayer to pray.

SUNSHINE

I heard her whisper: " Call me, will you, dear?
   They say Death parts, but I won't go away.
I will be with you in the cabin here;
   Oh, I will plead with God to let me stay!
Stay till the Night is gone, till Spring is nigh,
Till sunshine comes . . . be brave . . . I'm tired
    . . . good-bye . . ."

X.

For weeks, for months I have not seen the sun;
   The minatory dawns are leprous pale;
The felon days malinger one by one;
    How like a dream Life is! how vain! how
      stale!
I, too, am faint; that vampire-like disease
   Has fallen on me; weak and cold am I,
Hugging a tiny fire in fear I freeze:
    The cabin must be cold, and so I try
To bear the frost, the frost that fights decay,
The frost that keeps her beautiful alway.

XI.

She lies within an icy vault;
It glitters like a cave of salt.

SUNSHINE

All marble-pure and angel-sweet
With candles at her head and feet,
Under an ermine robe she lies.
I kiss her hands, I kiss her eyes:
" Come back, come back, O Love, I pray,
Into this house, this house of clay!
Answer my kisses soft and warm;
Nestle again within my arm.
Come! for I know that you are near;
Open your eyes and look, my dear.
Just for a moment break the mesh;
Back from the spirit leap to flesh.
Weary I wait; the night is black;
Love of my life, come back, come back!"

XII.

Last night maybe I was a little mad,
  For as I prayed despairful by her side,
Such a strange, antic visioning I had:
  Lo! it did seem *her eyes were open wide.*
Surely I must have dreamed! I stared once
       more . . .
  No, 'twas a candle's trick, a shadow cast.
There were her lashes locking as before.
  (Oh, but it filled me with a joy so vast!)
No, 'twas a freak, a fancy of the brain.
  (Oh, but to-night I'll try again, again!)

SUNSHINE

XIII.

It was no dream; now do I know that Love
　　Leapt from the starry battlements of Death;
For in my vigil as I bent above,
　　Calling her name with eager, burning breath,
Sudden there came a change; again I saw
　　The radiance of the rose-leaf stain her cheek;
Rivers of rapture thrilled in sunny thaw;
　　Cleft were her coral lips as if to speak;
Curved were her tender arms as if to cling;
　　Open the flower-like eyes of lucent blue,
Looking at me with love so pitying
　　That I could fancy Heaven shining through.
" Sunshine," I faltered, " stay with me, oh,
　　　　stay !"
Yet ere I finished, in a moment's flight,
There in her angel purity she lay—
　　Ah! but I know she'll come again to-night.
Even as radiant sword leaps from the sheath,
Soul from the body leaps—we call it Death.

XIV.

　　Even as this line I write,
　　　　Do I know that she is near;
　　Happy am I, every night
　　　　Comes she back to bid me **cheer;**
　　Kissing her, I hold her fast;
　　Win her into life at last.

SUNSHINE

Did I dream that yesterday
  On yon mountain ridge a glow
Soft as moonstone paled away,
  Leaving less forlorn the snow?
Could it be the sun? Oh, fain
Would I see the sun again!

Oh, to see a coral dawn
  Gladden to a crocus glow!
Day's a spectre dim and wan,
  Dancing on the furtive snow;
Night's a cloud upon my brain:
Oh, to see the sun again!

You who find us in this place,
  Have you pity in your breast;
Let us in our last embrace
  Under earth sun-hallowed rest.
Night's a claw upon my brain:
Oh, to see the sun again!

XV.

The Sun! at last the Sun! I write these lines,
  Here on my knees, with feeble, fumbling
        hand.
Look! in yon mountain cleft a radiance shines,
  Gleam of a primrose—see it thrill, expand,

41

SUNSHINE

Grow   glorious.   Dear God be praised! it
    streams
  Into the cabin in a gush of gold.
Look! there she stands, the angel of my dreams,
  All in the radiant shimmer aureoled;
First as I saw her from my bed of pain;
  First as I loved her when the darkness
    passed.
Now do I know that Life is not in vain;
  Now do I know God cares, at last, at last!
Light outlives dark, joy grief, and Love's the
    sum:
Heart of my heart! Sunshine! I come . . . I
    come . . .

THE IDEALIST

Oh, you who have daring deeds to tell!
And you who have felt Ambition's spell!
Have you heard of the louse who longed to dwell
    In the golden hair of a queen?
He sighed all day and he sighed all night,
And no one could understand it quite,
For the head of a slut is a louse's delight,
    But he pined for the head of a queen.

So he left his kinsfolk in merry play,
And off by his lonesome he stole away,
From the home of his youth so bright and gay,
    And gloriously unclean.
And at last he came to the palace gate,
And he made his way in a manner straight
(For a louse may go where a man must wait)
    To the tiring-room of the queen.

43

THE IDEALIST

The queen she spake to her tiring-maid:
" There's something the matter, I'm afraid.
To-night ere for sleep my hair ye braid,
    Just see what may be seen."
And lo, when they combed that shining hair,
They found him alone in his glory there,
And he cried: " I die, but I do not care,
    For I've lived in the head of a queen!"

ATHABASKA DICK

WHEN the boys come out from Lac Labiche in
    the lure of the early Spring,
  To take the pay of the "Hudson's Bay," as
    their fathers did before,
They are all aglee for the jamboree, and they
    make the Landing ring
  With a whoop and a whirl, and a "Grab your
    girl," and a rip and a skip and a roar.
For the spree of Spring is a sacred thing, and
    the boys must have their fun;
  Packer and tracker and half-breed Cree, from
    the boat to the bar they leap;
And then when the long flotilla goes, and the
    last of their pay is done,
  The boys from the banks of Lac Labiche
    swing to the heavy sweep.
And oh, how they sigh! and their throats are
    dry, and sorry are they and sick:
Yet there's none so cursed with a lime-kiln
    thirst as that Athabaska Dick.

ATHABASKA DICK

He was long and slim and lean of limb, but
    strong as a stripling bear;
  And by the right of his skill and might he
    guided the Long Brigade.
All water-wise were his laughing eyes, and he
    steered with a careless care,
  And he shunned the shock of foam and rock,
    till they came to the Big Cascade.
And here they must make the long *portage,* and
    the boys sweat in the sun;
  And they heft and pack, and they haul and
    track, and each must do his trick;
But their thoughts are far in the Landing bar,
    where the founts of nectar run:
  And no man thinks of such gorgeous drinks
    as that Athabaska Dick.

'Twas the close of day, and his long boat lay
    just over the Big Cascade,
  When there came to him one Jack-pot Jim,
    with a wild light in his eye;
And he softly laughed, and he led Dick aft, all
    eager, yet half afraid,
  And snugly stowed in his coat he showed a
    pilfered flask of " rye."

46

ATHABASKA DICK

And in haste he slipped, or in fear he tripped,
        but—Dick in warning roared—
    And there rang a yell, and it befell that Jim
        was overboard.

Oh, I heard a splash, and quick as a flash I knew
        he could not swim.
    I saw him whirl in the river swirl, and thresh
        his arms about.
In a queer, strained way I heard Dick say:
        " I'm going after him,"
    Throw off his coat, leap down the boat—and
        then I gave a shout:
" Boys, grab him, quick! You're crazy, Dick!
        Far better one than two!
    Hell, man! You know you've got no show!
        It's sure and certain death . . . "
And there we hung, and there we clung, with
        beef and brawn and thew,
    And sinews cracked and joints were racked,
        and panting came our breath;
And there we swayed and there we prayed, till
        strength and hope were spent—
Then Dick, he threw us off like rats and after
        Jim he went.

ATHABASKA DICK

With a mighty urge amid the surge of river-
　　rage he leapt,
　And gripped his mate and desperate he
　　　fought to gain the shore;
With teeth agleam he bucked the stream, yet
　　swift and sure he swept
　To meet the mighty cataract that waited all
　　　aroar.
And there we stood like carven wood, our faces
　　sickly white,
　And watched him as he beat the foam, and
　　　inch by inch he lost;
And nearer, nearer drew the fall, and fiercer
　　grew the fight,
　Till on the very cascade crest a last farewell
　　　he tossed.
Then down and down and down they plunged
　　into that pit of dread;
And mad we tore along the shore to claim our
　　bitter dead.

And from that hell of frenzied foam, that
　　crashed and fumed and boiled,
　Two little bodies bubbled up, and they were
　　　heedless then;

ATHABASKA DICK

And oh, they lay like senseless clay! and bitter
    hard we toiled,
    Yet never, never gleam of hope, and we were
        weary men.
And moments mounted into hours, and black
    was our despair;
    And faint were we, and we were fain to give
        them up as dead,
When suddenly I thrilled with hope: "Back,
    boys! and give him air;
I feel the flutter of his heart . . ." And, as
    the word I said,
Dick gave a sigh, and gazed around, and saw our
    breathless band;
    And saw the sky's blue floor above, all strewn
        with golden fleece;
And saw his comrade Jack-pot Jim, and
    touched him with his hand;
    And then there came into his eyes a look of
        perfect peace.
And as there, at his very feet, the thwarted
    river raved,
I heard him murmur low and deep: "Thank
    God! the *whiskey's* saved."

CHEER

It's a mighty good world, so it is, dear lass,
    When even the worst is said.
There's a smile and a tear, a sigh and a cheer,
    But better be living than dead;
A joy and a pain, a loss and a gain;
    There's honey and maybe some gall:
Yet still I declare, foul weather or fair,
    It's a mighty good world after all.

For look, lass! at night when I break from the
        fight,
    My Kingdom's awaiting for me;
There's comfort and rest, and the warmth of
        your breast,
    And little ones climbing my knee.
There's fire-light and song—Oh, the world may
        be wrong,
    Its empires may topple and fall:
My home is my care—if gladness be there,
    It's a mighty good world after all.

CHEER

O heart of pure gold! I have made you a fold,
   It's sheltered, sun-fondled and warm.
O little ones, rest! I have fashioned a nest;
   Sleep on! you are safe from the storm.
For there's no foe like fear, and there's no
         friend like cheer,
   And sunshine will flash at our call;
So crown Love as King, and let us all sing—
   "It's a mighty good world after all."

THE RETURN

THEY turned him loose; he bowed his head,
　A felon, bent and grey.
His face was even as the Dead,
　He had no word to say.

He sought the home of his old love,
　To look on her once more;
And where her roses breathed above,
　He cowered beside the door.

She sat there in the shining room;
　Her hair was silver grey.
He stared and stared from out the gloom:
　He turned to go away.

Her roses rustled overhead.
　She saw, with sudden start.
"I knew that you would come," she said.
　And held him to her heart.

THE RETURN

Her face was rapt and angel-sweet;
She touched his hair of grey;

.   .   .   .

But he, sob-shaken, at her feet,
Could only pray and pray.

THE JUNIOR GOD

THE Junior God looked from his place
  In the conning-towers of heaven,
And he saw the world through the span of space
  Like a giant golf-ball driven.
And because he was bored, as some gods are,
  With high celestial mirth,
He clutched the reins of a shooting star,
  And he steered it down to earth.

The Junior God, 'mid leaf and bud,
  Passed on with a weary air,
Till lo! he came to a pool of mud,
  And some hogs were rolling there.
Then in he plunged with gleeful cries,
  And down he lay supine;
For they had no mud in paradise,
  And they likewise had no swine.

54

THE JUNIOR GOD

The Junior God forgot himself;
  He squelched mud through his toes;
With the careless joy of a wanton boy
  His reckless laughter rose.
Till, tired at last, in a brook close by,
  He washed off every stain;
Then softly up to the radiant sky
  He rose, a god again.

The Junior God now heads the roll
  In the list of heaven's peers;
He sits in the House of High Control,
  And he regulates the spheres.
Yet does he wonder, do you suppose,
  If, even in gods divine,
The best and wisest may not be those
  Who have wallowed awhile with the swine?

THE NOSTOMANIAC

On the ragged edge of the world I'll roam,
And the home of the wolf shall be my home,
And a bunch of bones on the boundless snows
The end of my trail . . . who knows, who knows!

I'm dreaming to-night in the fire-glow, alone in
    my study tower,
  My books battalioned around me, my Kipling
    flat on my knee;
But I'm not in the mood for reading, I haven't
    moved for an hour;
  Body and brain I'm weary, weary the heart
    of me;
Weary of crushing a longing it's little I under-
    stand,
  For I thought that my trail was ended, I
    thought I had earned my rest;
But oh, it's stronger than life is, the call of the
    hearthless land!
  And I turn to the North in my trouble, as a
    child to the mother-breast.

THE NOSTOMANIAC

Here in my den it's quiet; the sea-wind taps on
    the pane;
  There's comfort and ease and plenty, the
    smile of the South is sweet.
All that a man might long for, fight for and
    seek in vain,
  Pictures and books and music, pleasure my
    last retreat.
Peace! I thought I had gained it, I swore that
    my tale was told;
  By my hair that is grey I swore it, by my
    eyes that are slow to see;
Yet what does it all avail me? to-night, to-night
    as of old,
  Out of the dark I hear it—the Northland
    calling to me.

And I'm daring a rampageous river that runs
    the devil knows where;
  My hand is athrill on the paddle, the birch-
    bark bounds like a bird.
Hark to the rumble of rapids! Here in my
    morris chair,
  Eager and tense I'm straining—isn't it most
    absurd?

THE NOSTOMANIAC

Now in the churn and the lather, foam that
       hisses and stings,
  Leap I, keyed for the struggle, fury and fume
      and roar;
Rocks are spitting like hell-cats—Oh, it's a sport
       for kings,
  Life on a twist of the paddle .   .   .   there's
      my " Kim" on the floor.

How I thrill and I vision! Then my camp of a
       night;
  Red and gold of the fire-glow, net afloat in
      the stream;
Scent of the pines and silence, little " pal " pipe
      alight,
  Body a-purr with pleasure, sleep untroubled
      of dream:
Banquet of paystreak bacon! moment of joy
      divine,
  When the bannock is hot and gluey, and the
      teapot's nearing the boil!
Never was wolf so hungry, stomach cleaving to
      spine . . .
  Ha! there's my servant calling, says that
      dinner will spoil.

THE NOSTOMANIAC

What do I want with dinner? Can I eat any
    more?
  Can I sleep as I used to? . . . Oh, I abhor this
    life!
Give me the Great Uncertain, the Barren Land
    for a floor,
  The Milky Way for a roof-beam, splendour
    and space and strife:
Something to fight and die for—the limpid
    Lake of the Bear,
  The Empire of Empty Bellies, the dunes
    where the Dogribs dwell;
Big things, real things, live things . . . here in
    my morris chair,
  How I ache for the Northland! "Dinner
    and servants"—Hell!

Am I too old, I wonder? Can I take one trip
    more?
  Go to the granite-ribbed valleys, flooded with
    sunset wine,
Peaks that pierce the aurora, rivers I must
    explore,
  Lakes of a thousand islands, millioning
    hordes of the Pine?

THE NOSTOMANIAC

Do they miss me, I wonder, valley and **peak** and
    plain?
  Whispering each to the other: " Many a moon
    has passed . . .
Where has he gone, our lover? Will he come
    back again?
  Star with his fires our tundra, leave us his
    bones at last?"

Yes, I'll go back to the Northland, back to **the**
    way of the bear,
  Back to the muskeg and mountain, back to
    the ice-leaguered sea.
Old am I! What does it matter? Nothing I
    would not dare;
  Give me a trail to conquer—Oh, it is " meat "
    to me!
I will go back to the Northland, feeble **and**
    blind and lame;
Sup with the sunny-eyed Husky, eat moose-nose
    with the Cree;
Play with the Yellow-knife bastards, boasting
    my blood and my name:
  I will go back to the Northland, for **the**
    Northland is calling to me.

THE NOSTOMANIAC

Then give to me paddle and whiplash, and give
    to me tumpline and gun;
  Give to me salt and tobacco, flour and a
    gunny of tea;
Take me up over the Circle, under the flam-
    boyant sun;
  Turn me foot-loose like a savage—that is the
    finish of me.
I know the trail I am seeking, it's up by the
    Lake of the Bear;
  It's down by the Arctic Barrens, it's over to
    Hudson's Bay;
Maybe I'll get there—maybe: death is set by a
    hair . . .
  Hark! it's the Northland calling! now must
    I go away . . .

  Go to the Wild that waits for me;
  Go where the moose and the musk-ox be;
  Go to the wolf and the secret snows;
  Go to my fate . . . who knows, who knows!

AMBITION

THEY brought the mighty chief to town;
  They showed him strange, unwonted sights;
Yet as he wandered up and down,
  He seemed to scorn their vain delights.
His face was grim, his eye lacked fire,
  As one who mourns a glory dead;
And when they sought his heart's desire:
  " Me like-um tooth same gold," he said.

A dental place they quickly found.
  He neither moaned nor moved his head.
They pulled his teeth so white and sound;
  They put in teeth of gold instead.
Oh, never saw I man so gay,
  His very being seemed to swell:
" Ha, ha !" he cried, " Now Injun say
  Me heap big chief, *me look like hell!*"

TO SUNNYDALE

THERE lies the trail to Sunnydale,
  Amid the lure of laughter.
Oh, how can we unhappy be
  Beneath its leafy rafter!
Each perfect hour is like a flower,
  Each day is like a posy.
How can you say the skies are grey?
  You're wrong, my friend, they're rosy.

With right good will let's climb the hill,
  And leave behind all sorrow.
Oh, we'll be gay! a bright to-day
  Will make a bright to-morrow.
Oh, we'll be strong! the way is long
  That never has a turning;
The hill is high, but there's the sky,
  And how the West is burning!

TO SUNNYDALE

And if through chance of circumstance
  We have to go bare-foot, sir,
We'll not repine—a friend of mine
  Has got no feet to boot, sir.
This Happiness a habit is,
  And Life is what we make it:
See! there's the trail to Sunnydale!
  Up, friend! and let us take it.

THE BLIND AND THE DEAD

SHE lay like a saint on her copper couch;
   Like an angel asleep she lay,
In the stare of the ghoulish folks that slouch
   Past the Dead and sneak away.

Then came old Jules of the sightless gaze,
   Who begged in the streets for bread.
Each day he had come for a year of days,
   And groped his way to the Dead.

"What's the Devil's Harvest to-day?" he cried;
   "A wanton with eyes of blue!
I've known too many a such," he sighed;
   " Maybe I know this . . . mon Dieu!"

He raised the head of the heedless Dead;
   He fingered the frozen face . . .
Then a deathly spell on the watchers fell—
   God! it was still, that place!

THE BLIND AND THE DEAD

He raised the head of the careless **Dead**;
  He fumbled a vagrant curl;
And then with his sightless smile he **said**:
  " It's only my little girl."

" Dear, my dear, did they hurt you **so**!
  Come to your daddy's heart . . . "
Aye, and he held so tight, you know,
  They were hard to force apart.

No! Paris isn't always **gay**;
  And the morgue has its stories, **too**:
You are a writer of tales, you say—
  Then there is a tale **for you**.

THE ATAVIST

WHAT are you doing here, Tom Thorne, on the
      white top-knot of the world,
  Where the wind has the cut of a naked knife
      and the stars are rapier keen?
Hugging a smudgy willow fire, deep in a lynx
      robe curled,
  You that's a lord's own son, Tom Thorne—
      what does your madness mean?

Go home, go home to your clubs, Tom Thorne!
      home to your evening dress!
  Home to your place of power and pride, and
      the feast that waits for you!
Why do you linger all alone in the splendid
      emptiness,
  Scouring the Land of the Little Sticks on the
      trail of the caribou?

THE ATAVIST

Why did you fall off the Earth, Tom Thorne,
    out of our social ken?
  What did your deep damnation prove? What
    was your dark despair?
Oh, with the width of a world between, and years
    to the count of ten,
  If they cut out your heart to-night, Tom
    Thorne, *her* name would be graven
    there.

And you fled afar for the thing called Peace,
    and you thought you would find it
    here,
  In the purple tundras vastly spread, and the
    mountains whitely piled;
It's a weary quest and a dreary quest, but I
    think that the end is near;
  For they say that the Lord has hidden it in
    the secret heart of the Wild.

And you know that heart as few men know, and
    your eyes are fey and deep,
  With a " something lost " come welling back
    from the raw, red dawn of life:
With woe and pain have you greatly lain, till
    out of abysmal sleep
  The soul of the Stone Age leaps in you, alert
    for the ancient strife.

THE ATAVIST

And if you came to our feast again, with its
            pomp and glee and glow,
    I think you would sit stone-still, Tom Thorne,
            and see in a daze of dream
A mad sun goading to frenzied flame the glitter-
            ing gems of the snow,
    And a monster musk-ox bulking black against
            the blood-red gleam.

I think you would see berg-battling shores, and
            stammer and halt and stare
    With a sudden sense of the frozen void,
            serene and vast and still;
And the aching gleam and the hush of dream,
            and the track of a great white bear,
    And the primal lust that surged in you as you
            sprang to make your kill.

I think you would hear the bull-moose call, and
            the glutted river roar,
    And spy the hosts of the caribou shadow the
            shining plain;
And feel the pulse of the silences, and stand
            elate once more
    On the verge of the yawning vastitudes that
            call to you in vain.

THE ATAVIST

For I think you are one with the stars and the
    sun, and the wind and the wave and the
    dew;
  And the peaks untrod that yearn to God, and
    the valleys undefiled;
Men soar with wings, and they bridle kings, but
    what is it all to you,
  Wise in the ways of the wilderness, and strong
    with the strength of the Wild?

You have spent your life, you have waged your
    strife where never we play a part;
  You have held the throne of the Great
    Unknown, you have ruled a kingdom
    vast:

     .   .   .   .

*But to-night there's a strange, new trail for you,
    and you go, O weary heart!*
  *To the peace and rest of the Great Unguessed
    . . . at last, Tom Thorne, at last.*

THE SCEPTIC

My Father Christmas passed away
   When I was barely seven.
At twenty-one, alack-a-day,
   I lost my hope of heaven.

Yet not in either lies the curse:
   The hell of it's because
I don't know which loss hurt the worse—
   My God or Santa Claus.

THE ROVER

I.

Oh, how good it is to be
Foot-loose and heart-free!
Just my dog and pipe and I, underneath the
vast sky;
Trail to try and goal to win, white road and cool
inn;
Fields to lure a lad afar, clear spring and still
star;
Lilting feet that never tire, green dingle, faggot
fire;
None to hurry, none to hold, heather hill and
hushed fold;
Nature like a picture-book, laughing leaf and
bright brook;
Every day a jewel bright, set serenely in the
night;
Every night a holy shrine, radiant for a day
divine.

THE ROVER

Weathered cheek and kindly eye, let the wan-
     derer go by.
Woman-love and wistful heart, let the gipsy one
     depart.
For the farness and the road are his glory and
     his goad.
Oh, the lilt of youth and Spring! Eyes laugh
     and lips sing.
        Yea, but it is good to be
        Foot-loose and heart-free!

II.

        Yet how good it is to come
        Home at last, home, home!
On the clover swings the bee, overhead's the hale
     tree.
Sky of turquoise gleams through, yonder glints
     the lake's blue.
In a hammock let's swing, weary of wandering;
Tired of wild, uncertain lands, strange faces,
     faint hands.
Has the wondrous world gone cold? Am I grow-
     ing old, old?
Grey and weary . . .   let me dream, glide on
     the tranquil stream.

THE ROVER

Oh, what joyous days I've had, full, fervid, gay,
     glad!
Yet there comes a subtle change, let the strip-
     ling rove, range.
From sweet roving comes sweet rest, after all,
     home's best.
And if there's a little bit of woman-love with it,
I will count my life content, God-blest ard well
     spent . . .
        Oh, but it is good to be
        Foot-loose and heart-free!
        Yet how good it is to come
        Home at last, home, home!

BARB-WIRE BILL

At dawn of day the white land lay all gruesome-
      like and grim,
When Bill McGee he says to me: " We've *got* to
      do it, Jim.
We've got to make Fort Liard quick. I know
      the river's bad,
But, oh! the little woman's sick . . . why!
      don't you savvy, lad?"
And me! Well, yes, I must confess it wasn't
      hard to see
Their little family group of two would soon be
      one of three.
And so I answered, careless-like: " Why, Bill!
      you don't suppose
I'm scared of that there ' babbling brook '?
      Whatever you say—goes."

A real live man was Barb-wire Bill, with insides
      copper-lined;
For " barb-wire " was the brand of " hooch " to
      which he most inclined.

BARB-WIRE BILL

They knew him far; his igloos are on Kittie-
    gazuit strand.
They knew him well, the tribes who dwell within
    the Barren Land.
From Koyokuk to Kuskoquim his fame was
    everywhere;
And he did love, all life above, that little Julie
    Claire,
The lithe, white slave-girl he had bought for
    seven hundred skins,
And taken to his wickiup to make his moccasins.

We crawled down to the river bank, and feeble
    folk were we,
That Julie Claire from God-knows-where, and
    Barb-wire Bill and me.
From shore to shore we heard the roar the heav-
    ing ice-floes make,
And loud we laughed, and launched our raft,
    and followed in their wake.
The river swept and seethed and leapt, and
    caught us in its stride;
And on we hurled amid a world that crashed on
    every side.
With sullen din the banks caved in; the shore-
    ice lanced the stream;

BARB-WIRE BILL

The naked floes like spooks arose, all jigging and
    agleam.
Black anchor-ice of strange device shot upward
    from its bed,
As night and day we cleft our way, and arrow-
    like we sped.

But "Faster still!" cried Barb-wire Bill, and
    looked the live-long day
In dull despair at Julie Claire, where white like
    death she lay.
And sometimes he would seem to pray and some-
    times seem to curse,
And bent above, with eyes of love, yet ever she
    grew worse.
And as we plunged and leapt and lunged, her
    face was plucked with pain,
And I could feel his nerves of steel a-quiver at
    the strain.
And in the night he gripped me tight as I lay
    fast asleep:
"The river's kicking like a steer . . . run
    out the forward sweep!
That's Hell-gate Canyon right ahead; I know of
    old its roar,
And . . . I'll be damned! *the ice is jammed!*
    We've got to make the shore."

BARB-WIRE BILL

With one wild leap I gripped the sweep. The
    night was black as sin.
The float-ice crashed and ripped and smashed,
    and stunned us with its din.
And near and near, and clear and clear I heard
    the canyon boom;
And swift and strong we swept along to meet
    our awful doom.
And as with dread I glimpsed ahead the death
    that waited there,
My only thought was of the girl, the little Julie
    Claire;
And so, like demon mad with fear, I panted at
    the oar,
And foot by foot, and inch by inch, we worked
    the raft ashore.

The bank was staked with grinding ice, and as
    we scraped and crashed,
I only knew one thing to do, and through my
    mind it flashed:
Yet while I groped to find the rope, I heard Bill's
    savage cry:
"That's my job, lad! It's me that jumps. I'll
    snub this raft or die!"

BARB-WIRE BILL

I saw him leap, I saw him creep, I saw him gain
     the land;
I saw him crawl, I saw him fall, then run with
     rope in hand.
And then the darkness gulped him up, and down
     we dashed once more,
And nearer, nearer drew the jam, and thunder-
     like its roar.
Oh, God! all's lost . . . from Julie Claire
     there came a wail of pain,
And then—the rope grew sudden taut, and quiv-
     ered at the strain;
It slacked and slipped, it whined and gripped,
     and oh, I held my breath!
And there we hung and there we swung right in
     the jaws of death.

A little strand of hempen rope, and how I
     watched it there,
With all around a hell of sound, and darkness
     and despair;
A little strand of hempen rope, I watched it all
     alone,
And somewhere in the dark behind I heard a
     woman moan;

BARB-WIRE BILL

And somewhere in the dark ahead I heard a man
    cry out,
Then silence, silence, silence fell, and mocked
    my hollow shout.
And yet once more from out the shore I heard
    that cry of pain,
A moan of mortal agony, then all was still again.

That night was hell with all the frills, and when
    the dawn broke dim,
I saw a lean and level land, but never sign of
    him.
I saw a flat and frozen shore of hideous device,
I saw a long-drawn strand of rope that vanished
    through the ice.
And on that treeless, rockless shore I found my
    partner—dead.
No place was there to snub the raft, so—*he had
    served instead!*
And with the rope lashed round his waist, in
    last defiant fight,
He'd thrown himself beneath the ice, that closed
    and gripped him tight;
And there he'd held us back from death, as fast
    in death he lay . . .
Say, boys! I'm not the pious brand, but—I just
    tried to pray.

BARB-WIRE BILL

And then I looked to Julie Claire, and sore
     abashed was I,
For from the robes that covered her *I heard—a*
     baby cry. . . .

   .   .   .   .

Thus was Love conqueror of death, and life for
     life was given;
And though no saint on earth, d'ye think Bill's
     squared hisself with Heaven?

"?"

If you had the choice of two women to wed,
  (Though of course the idea is quite absurd),
And the first from her heels to her dainty head
  Was charming in every sense of the word:
And yet in the past (I grieve to state)
She never had been exactly " straight."

And the second—she was beyond all cavil,
  A model of virtue, I must confess;
And yet, alas! she was dull as the devil,
  And rather a dowd in the way of dress;
Though what she was lacking in wit and beauty
She more than made up for in " sense of duty."

Now, suppose you must wed, and make no blun-
      der,
  And either would love you, and let you win
      her—
Which of the two would you choose, I wonder,
  The stolid saint or the sparkling sinner?

JUST THINK!

Just think! some night the stars will gleam
    Upon a cold, grey stone,
And trace a name with silver beam,
    And lo! 'twill be your own.

That night is speeding on to greet
    Your epitaphic rhyme.
Your life is but a little beat
    Within the heart of Time.

A little gain, a little pain,
    A laugh, lest you may moan;
A little blame, a little fame,
    A star-gleam on a stone.

THE LUNGER

JACK would laugh an' joke all day;
Never saw a lad so gay;
Singin' like a medder lark,
Loaded to the Plimsoll mark
With God's sunshine was that boy;
Had a strangle-holt on Joy.
Held his head 'way up in air,
Left no callin'-cards on Care;
Breezy, buoyant, brave and true;
Sent his sunshine out to you;
Cheerfulest when clouds was black—
    Happy Jack! Oh, Happy Jack!

Sittin' in my shack alone
I could hear him in his own,
Singin' far into the night,
Till it didn't seem just right
One man should corral the fun,
Live his life so in the sun;
Didn't seem quite natural
Not to have a grouch at all;
Not a trouble, not a lack—
    Happy Jack! Oh, Happy Jack!

THE LUNGER

He was plumbful of good cheer
Till he struck that low-down year;
Got so thin, so little to him,
You could most see daylight through him.
Never was his eye so bright,
Never was his cheek so white.
Seemed as if somethin' was wrong,
Sort o' quaver in his song.
Same old smile, same hearty voice:
" Bless you, boys! let's all rejoice!"
But old Doctor shook his head:
" Half a lung," was all he said.
Yet that half was surely right,
For I heard him every night,
Singin', singin' in his shack—
   Happy Jack! Oh, Happy Jack!

Then one day a letter came
Endin' with a female name;
Seemed to get him in the neck,
Sort o' pile-driver effect;
Paled his lip and plucked his breath,
Left him starin' still as death.
Somethin' had gone awful wrong,
Yet that night he sang his song.
Oh, but it was good to hear!
For there clutched my heart a fear,

THE LUNGER

So that I quaked listenin'
Every night to hear him sing.
But each day he laughed with me,
An' his smile was full of glee.
Nothin' seemed to set him back—
    Happy Jack! Oh, Happy Jack!

Then one night the singin' stopped . . .
Seemed as if my heart just flopped;
For I'd learned to love the boy
With his gilt-edged line of joy,
With his glorious gift of bluff,
With his splendid fightin' stuff.
Sing on, lad, and play the game!
O dear God! . . . no singin' came,
But there surged to me instead—
Silence, silence, deep and dread;
Till I shuddered, tried to pray,
Said: "He's maybe gone away."

Oh, yes, he had gone away,
Gone forever and a day.
But he'd left behind him there,
In his cabin, pinched and bare,
His poor body, skin and bone,
His sharp face, cold as a stone.

THE LUNGER

An' his stiffened fingers pressed
Somethin' bright upon his breast:
Locket with a silken curl,
Poor, sweet portrait of a girl.
Yet I reckon at the last
How defiant-like he passed;
For there sat upon his lips
Smile that death could not eclipse;
An' within his eyes lived still
Joy that dyin' could not kill.

An' now when the nights are long,
How I miss his cheery song!
How I sigh an' wish him back!
  Happy Jack! Oh, Happy Jack!

THE MOUNTAIN AND THE LAKE

I KNOW a mountain thrilling to the stars,
  Peerless and pure, and pinnacled with snow;
Glimpsing the golden dawn o'er coral bars,
  Flaunting the vanisht sunset's garnet glow;
Proudly patrician, passionless, serene;
  Soaring in silvered steeps where cloud-surfs
      break;
Virgin and vestal—Oh, a very Queen!
  And at her feet there dreams a quiet lake.

My lake adores my mountain—well I know,
  For I have watched it from its dawn-dream
      start,
Stilling its mirror to her splendid snow,
  Framing her image in its trembling heart;
Glassing her graciousness of greening wood,
  Kissing her throne, melodiously mad,
Thrilling responsive to her every mood,
  Gloomed with her sadness, gay when she is
      glad.

THE MOUNTAIN AND THE LAKE

My lake has dreamed and loved since time was
     born;
  Will love and dream till time shall cease to be;
Gazing to Her in worship half forlorn,
  Who looks towards the stars and will not see—
My peerless mountain, splendid in her scorn. . . .
  Alas! poor little lake! Alas! poor me!

THE HEADLINER AND THE
BREADLINER

Moko, the Educated Ape, is here,
  The pet of vaudeville, so the posters say,
  And every night the gaping people pay
To see him in his panoply appear;
To see him pad his paunch with dainty cheer,
  Puff his perfecto, swill champagne, and sway
  Just like a gentleman, yet all in play,
Then bow himself off stage with brutish leer.

And as to-night, with noble knowledge crammed,
  I 'mid this human compost take my place,
I, once a poet, now so dead and damned,
  The woeful tears half freezing on my face:
" O God!" I cry, " let me but take his shape,
  Moko's, the Blest, the Educated Ape."

DEATH IN THE ARCTIC

i.

I took the clock down from the shelf;
" At eight," said I, " I shoot myself."
It lacked a *minute* of the hour,
And as I waited all a-cower,
A skinful of black, boding pain,
Bits of my life came back again. . . .

" *Mother, there's nothing more to eat—*
Why don't you go out on the street?
Always you sit and cry and cry;
Here at my play I wonder why.
Mother, when you dress up at night,
Red are your cheeks, your eyes are bright;
Twining a riband in your hair,
Kissing good-bye you go down-stair.
Then I'm as lonely as can be.
Oh, how I wish you were with me!
Yet when you go out on the street,
Mother, there's always lots to eat." . . .

DEATH IN THE ARCTIC

II.

For days the igloo has been dark;
But now the rag wick sends a spark
That glitters in the icy air,
And wakes frost sapphires everywhere;
Bright, bitter flames, that adder-like
Dart here and there, yet fear to strike
The gruesome gloom wherein *they* lie,
My comrades, oh, so keen to die!
And I, the last—well, here I wait
The clock to strike the hour of eight. . . .

" Boy, it is bitter to be hurled
Nameless and naked on the world;
Frozen by night and starved by day,
Curses and kicks and clouts your pay.
But you must fight! Boy, look on me!
Anarch of all earth-misery;
Beggar and tramp and shameless sot;
Emblem of ill, in rags that rot.
Would you be foul and base as I?
Oh, it is better far to die!
Swear to me now you'll fight and fight,
Boy, or I'll kill you here to-night." . . .

DEATH IN THE ARCTIC

III.

Curse this silence soft and black!
Sting, little light, the shadows back!
Dance, little flame, with freakish glee!
Twinkle with brilliant mockery!
Glitter on ice-robed roof and floor!
Jewel the bear-skin of the door!
Gleam in my beard, illume my breath,
Blanch the clock face that times my death!
But do not pierce that murk so deep,
Where in their sleeping-bags they sleep!
But do not linger where they lie,
They who had all the luck to die!   .   .   .

" There is nothing more to say;
Let us part and go our way.
Since it seems we can't agree,
I will go across the sea.
Proud of heart and strong am I;
Not for woman will I sigh;
Hold my head up gay and glad:
You can find another lad."   .   .   .

IV.

Above the igloo piteous flies
Our frayed flag to the frozen skies.

DEATH IN THE ARCTIC

Oh, would you know how earth can be
A hell—go north of Eighty-three!
Go, scan the snows day after day,
And hope for help, and pray and pray;
Have seal-hide and sea-lice to eat;
Melt water with your body's heat;
Sleep all the fell, black winter through
Beside the dear, dead men you knew.
(The walrus blubber flares and gleams—
O God! how long a minute seems!) . . .

" *Mary, many a day has passed,*
   Since that morn of hot-head youth.
Come I back at last, at last,
   Crushed with knowing of the truth:
How through bitter, barren years
   You loved me, and me alone;
Waited, wearied, wept your tears—
Oh, could I atone, atone,
I would pay a million-fold!
   Pay you for the love you gave.
Mary, look down as of old—
   I am kneeling by your grave." . . .

DEATH IN THE ARCTIC

V.

Olaf, the Blonde, was the first to go;
Bitten his eyes were by the snow;
Sightless and sealed his eyes of blue,
So that he died before I knew.
Here in these poor weak arms he died:
" Wolves will not get you, lad," I lied;
" For I will watch till Spring come round;
Slumber you shall beneath the ground."
Oh, how I lied! I scarce can wait:
Strike, little clock, the hour of eight! . . .

" *Comrade, can you blame me quite?*
The horror of the long, long night
Is on me, and I've borne with pain
So long, and hoped for help in vain.
So frail am I, and blind and dazed;
With scurvy sick, with silence crazed.
Beneath the Arctic's heel of hate,
Avid for Death I wait, I wait.
Oh, if I falter, fail to fight,
Can you, dear comrade, blame me quite?"

VI.

Big Eric gave up months ago.
But seldom do men suffer so.

DEATH IN THE ARCTIC

His feet sloughed off, his fingers died,
His hands shrunk up and mummified.
I had to feed him like a child;
Yet he was valiant, joked and smiled,
Talked of his wife and little one
(Thanks be to God that I have none),
Passed in the night without a moan,
Passed, and I'm here, alone, alone. . . .

"I've got to kill you, Dick.
 Your life for mine, you know.
Better to do it quick,
 A swift and sudden blow.
See! here's my hand to lick;
 A hug before you go—
God! but it makes me sick;
 Old dog, I love you so.
Forgive, forgive me, Dick—
 A swift and sudden blow.". . .

VII.

Often I start up in the dark,
 Thinking the sound of bells to hear.
Often I wake from sleep: "Oh, hark!
 Help . . . it is coming . . . near
 and near."

DEATH IN THE ARCTIC

Blindly I reel toward the door;
  There the snow billows bleak and bare;
Blindly I seek my den once more,
  Silence and darkness and despair.
Oh, it is all a dreadful dream!
  Scurvy and cold and death and dearth;
I will awake to warmth and gleam,
  Silvery seas and greening earth.
Life is a dream, its wakening,
Death, gentle shadow of God's wing. . . .

" Tick, little clock, my life away!
  Even a second seems a day.
  Even a minute seems a year,
  Peopled with ghosts that press and peer
  Into my face so charnel white,
  Lit by the devilish, dancing light.
  Tick, little clock! mete out my fate:
  Tortured and tense I wait, I wait." . . .

VIII.

Oh, I have sworn! the hour is nigh:
When it strikes eight, I die, I die.

DEATH IN THE ARCTIC

Raise up the gun—it stings my brow—
When it strikes eight . . . all ready
    . . . *now*—

   *   *   *   *   *   *

Down from my hand the weapon dropped;
Wildly I stared . . .
    THE CLOCK HAD STOPPED.

IX.

Phantoms and fears and ghosts have gone.
  Peace seems to nestle in my brain.
Lo! the clock stopped, I'm living on;
  Heart-sick I was, and less than sane.
Yet do I scorn the thing I planned,
  Hearing a voice: "O coward, fight!"
Then the clock stopped . . . whose was
    the hand?
  Maybe 'twas God's—ah, well, all's right.
Heap on me darkness, fold on fold!
  Pain! wrench and rack me! What care I?
Leap on me, hunger, thirst and cold!
  I will await my time to die;
Looking to Heaven that shines above;
Looking to God, and love . . . and love.

98

DEATH IN THE ARCTIC

X.

Hark! what is that? Bells, dogs again!
  Is it a dream? I sob and cry.
See! the door opens, fur-clad men
  Rush to my rescue; frail am I;
Feeble and dying, dazed and glad.
  There is the pistol where it dropped.
" Boys, it was hard—but I'm not mad . . .
  Look at the clock—it stopped, it stopped.
Carry me out. The heavens smile.
  See! there's an arch of gold above.
Now, let me rest a little while—
  Looking to God and love . .. and love."

DREAMS ARE BEST

I JUST think that dreams are best,
   Just to sit and fancy things;
Give your gold no acid test,
   Try not how your silver rings;
Fancy women pure and good,
   Fancy men upright and true:
Fortressed in your solitude,
   Let Life be a dream to you.

For I think that Thought is all;
   Truth's a minion of the mind;
Love's ideal comes at call;
   As ye seek so shall ye find.
But ye must not seek too far;
   Things are never what they seem:
Let a star be just a star,
   And a woman—just a dream.

DREAMS ARE BEST

O you Dreamers, proud and pure,
  You have gleaned the sweet of life!
Golden truths that shall endure
  Over pain and doubt and strife.
I would rather be a fool
  Living in my Paradise,
Than the leader of a school,
  Sadly sane and weary-wise.

O you Cynics with your sneers,
  Fallen brains and hearts of brass,
Tweak me by my foolish ears,
  Write me down a simple ass!
I'll believe the real " you "
  Is the " you " without a taint;
I'll believe each woman, too,
  But a slightly damaged saint.

Yes, I'll smoke my cigarette,
  Vestured in my garb of dreams,
And I'll borrow no regret;
  All is gold that golden gleams.
So I'll charm my solitude
  With the faith that Life is blest,
Brave and noble, bright and good . . .
  Oh, I think that dreams are best!

THE QUITTER

WHEN you're lost in the Wild, and you're scared
    as a child,
  And Death looks you bang in the eye,
And you're sore as a boil, it's according to Hoyle
    To cock your revolver and . . . die.
But the Code of a Man says: "Fight all you
    can,"
  And self-dissolution is barred.
In hunger and woe, oh, it's easy to blow . . .
  It's the hell-served-for-breakfast that's hard.

"You're sick of the game!" Well, now, that's a
    shame.
    You're young and you're brave and you're
    bright.
"You've had a raw deal!" I know—but don't
    squeal,
    Buck up, do your damnedest, and fight.
It's the plugging away that will win you the day,
    So don't be a piker, old pard!
Just draw on your grit; it's so easy to quit:
    It's the keeping-your-chin-up that's hard.

THE QUITTER

It's easy to cry that you're beaten—and die;
  It's easy to crawfish and crawl;
But to fight and to fight when hope's out of
      sight—
  Why, that's the best game of them all!
And though you come out of each gruelling bout
  All broken and beaten and scarred,
Just have one more try—it's dead easy to die,
  It's the keeping-on-living that's hard.

THE COW-JUICE CURE

THE clover was in blossom, an' the year was at
the June,
When Flap-jack Billy hit the town, likewise
O'Flynn's saloon.
The frost was on the fodder an' the wind was
growin' keen,
When Billy got to seein' snakes in Sullivan's
shebeen.

Then in meandered Deep-hole Dan, once comrade of the cup:
"Oh, Billy, for the love of Mike, why don't ye
sober up?
I've got the gorgus recipay, 'tis smooth an' slick
as silk—
Jest quit yer strangle-holt on hooch, an' irrigate
with milk.
Lackteeal flooid is the lubrication you require;
Yer nervus frame-up's like a bunch of snarled
piano wire.

104

THE COW-JUICE CURE

You want to get it coated up with addypose
    tishoo,
So's it will work elastic-like, an' milk's the dope
    for you."

Well, Billy was complyable, an' in a month, it's
    strange,
That cow-juice seemed to oppyrate a most amaz-
    in' change.
" Call up the water-wagon, Dan, an' book my
    seat," sez he.
" 'Tis mighty queer," sez Deep-hole Dan, " 'twas
    just the same with me."
They shanghaied little Tom O'Shane, they
    cached him safe away,
An' though he objurgated some, they " cured "
    him night an' day;
An' pretty soon there came the change amazin'
    to explain:
" I'll never take another drink," sez Timothy
    O'Shane.
They tried it out on Spike Muldoon, that toper
    of renown;
They put it over Grouch McGraw, the terror of
    the town.

THE COW-JUICE CURE

They roped in " tanks " from far and near, an'
       every test was sure,
An' like a flame there ran the fame of Deep-
       hole's Cow-juice Cure.

" It's mighty queer," sez Deep-hole Dan, " I'm
       puzzled through and through;
It's only milk from Riley's ranch, no other milk
       will do."
An' it jest happened on that night, with no pre-
       dictive plan,
He left some milk from Riley's ranch a-settin'
       in a pan;
An' picture his amazement when he poured that
       milk next day—
There in the bottom of the pan a dozen " col-
       ours " lay.

" Well, what d'ye know 'bout that?" sez Dan;
       " Gosh-ding my dasted eyes,
We've been an' had the Gold Cure, Bill, an' none
       of us was wise!
The milk's free-millin', that's a cinch; there's
       colours everywhere.
Now, let us figger this thing out—how does the
       dust git there?

THE COW-JUICE CURE

' Gold from the grass-roots down,' they say—
    why, Bill! we've got it cold—
Them cows what nibbles up the grass, jest nib-
    bles up the gold.
We're blasted, bloomin' millionaires; dissemble
    an' lie low:
We'll follow them gold-bearin' cows, an' prospect
    where they go."

An' so it came to pass, fer weeks them miners
    might be found
A-sneakin' round on Riley's ranch, an' snipin'
    at the ground;
Till even Riley stops an' stares, an' presently
    allows:
" Them boys appear to take a mighty interest in
    cows."
An' night an' day they shadowed each aurifer-
    ous bovine,
An' panned the grass-roots on their trail, yet
    nivver gold they seen.
An' all that season, secret-like, they worked an'
    nothin' found;
An' there was colours in the milk, but none was
    in the ground.

THE COW-JUICE CURE

An' mighty desperate was they, an' down upon
    their luck,
When sudden, inspiration-like, the source of it
    they struck.
An' where d'ye think they traced it to? It
    grieves my heart to tell—
In the black sand at the bottom of that wicked
    milkman's *well*.

WHILE THE BANNOCK BAKES

LIGHT up your pipe again, old chum, and sit
    awhile with me;
  I've got to watch the bannock bake—how rest-
    ful is the air!
You'd little think that we were somewhere north
    of Sixty-three.
  Though where I don't exactly know, and don't
    precisely care.
The man-size mountains palisade us round on
    every side;
  The river is a-flop with fish, and ripples silver-
    clear;
The midnight sunshine brims yon cleft—we
    think it's the Divide;
  We'll get there in a month, maybe, or maybe
    in a year.

It doesn't matter, does it, pal? We're of that
    breed of men
  With whom the world of wine and cards and
    women disagree;

WHILE THE BANNOCK BAKES

Your trouble was a roofless game of poker now
    and then,
    And " raising up my elbow," that's what got
      away with me.
We're merely " Undesirables," artistic more or
    less;
    My horny hands are Chopin-wise; you quote
      your Browning well;
And yet we're fooling round for gold in this
    damned wilderness:
    The joke is, if we found it, we would both go
      straight to hell.

Well, maybe we won't find it—and at least we've
    got the " life."
    We're both as brown as berries, and could
      wrestle with a bear:
(That bannock's raising nicely, pal; just jab it
    with your knife.)
    Fine specimens of manhood they would reckon
      us out there.
It's the tracking and the packing and the poling
    in the sun;
    It's the sleeping in the open, it's the rugged,
      unfaked food;

WHILE THE BANNOCK BAKES

It's the snow-shoe and the paddle, and the camp-
    fire and the gun,
  And when I think of what I was, I know that
    it is good.

Just think of how we've poled all day up this
    strange little stream;
  Since life began no eye of man has seen this
    place before;
How fearless all the wild things are! the banks
    with goose-grass gleam,
  And there's a bronzy muskrat sitting sniffing
    at his door.
A mother duck with brood of ten comes squat-
    tering along;
  The tawny, white-winged ptarmigan are flying
    all about;
And in that swirly, golden pool, a restless, gleam-
    ing throng,
  The trout are waiting till we condescend to
    take them out.

Ah, yes, it's good! I'll bet that there's no doctor
    like the Wild:
  (Just turn that bannock over there; it's get-
    ting nicely brown):

111

WHILE THE BANNOCK BAKES

I might be in my grave by now, forgotten and
    reviled,
  Or rotting like a sickly cur in some far, for-
    eign town.
I might be that vile thing I was—it all seems
    like a dream;
  I owed a man a grudge one time that only life
    could pay;
And yet it's half-forgotten now—how petty these
    things seem!
  (But that's " another story," pal; I'll tell it
    you some day.)

How strange two " irresponsibles " should chum
    away up here!
  But round the Arctic Circle friends are few
    and far between.
We've shared the same camp-fire and tent for
    nigh on seven year,
  And never had a word that wasn't cheering
    and serene.
We've halved the toil and split the spoil, and
    borne each other's pack;
  By all the Wild's freemasonry we're brothers,
    tried and true;

WHILE THE BANNOCK BAKES

We've swept on danger side by side, and fought
    it back to back,
  And you would die for me, old pal, and I
    would die for you.

Now there was that time I got lost in Rory Bory
    Land,
  (How quick the blizzards sweep on one across
    that Polar sea!)
You formed a rescue crew of One, and saw a
    frozen hand
  That stuck out of a drift of snow—and, part-
    ner, it was Me.
But I got even, did I not, that day the paddle
    broke?
  White water on the Coppermine—a rock—a
    split canoe—
Two fellows struggling in the foam (one couldn't
    swim a stroke):
  A half-drowned man I dragged ashore . . .
    and, partner, it was You.

.   .   .   .

In Rory Borealis Land the winter's long and
    black;
  The silence seems a solid thing, shot through
    with wolfish woe;

113

WHILE THE BANNOCK BAKES

And rowelled by the eager stars the skies vault
  vastly back,
    And man seems but a little mite in that weird-
    lit plateau.
Nothing to do but smoke and yarn of wild and
  mis-spent lives,
    Beside the camp-fire there we sat—what tales
    you told to me
Of love and hate, and chance and fate, and tem-
  porary wives!
    In Rory Borealis Land, beside the Arctic Sea.

One yarn you told me in those days I can remem-
  ber still;
    It seemed as if I visioned it, so sharp you
    sketched it in;
Bellona was the name, I think; a coast town in
  Brazil,
    Where nobody did anything but serenade and
    sin.
I saw it all—the jewelled sea, the golden scythe
  of sand,
    The stately pillars of the palms, the feathery
    bamboo,

WHILE THE BANNOCK BAKES

The red-roofed houses and the swart, sun-dom-
    inated land,
The people ever children, and the heavens
    ever blue.

You told me of that girl of yours, that blossom
    of old Spain,
  All glamour, grace and witchery, all passion,
    verve and glow.
How maddening she must have been! You made
    me see her plain,
  There by our little camp-fire, in the silence
    and the snow.
You loved her and she loved you. She'd a hus-
    band, too, I think;
  A doctor chap, you told me, whom she treated
    like a dog,
A white man living on the beach, a hopeless
    slave to drink—
  (Just turn that bannock over there, that's
    propped against the log).

That story seemed to strike me, pal—it happens
    every day:
  You had to go away awhile, then somehow it
    befell

WHILE THE BANNOCK BAKES

The doctor chap discovered, gave her up, and
    went away;
  You came back, tired of her in time . . .
    there's nothing more to tell.
Hist! see those willows silvering where swamp
    and river meet!
  Just reach me up my rifle, quick; that's Mister
    Moose, I know—
There now, *I've got him dead to rights* . . .
    but, hell! we've lots to eat;
  I don't believe in taking life—we'll let the
    beggar go.

Heigh-ho! I'm tired; the bannock's cooked; it's
    time we both turned in.
  The morning mist is coral-kissed, the morning
    sky is gold.
The camp-fire's a confessional—what funny
    yarns we spin!
  It sort of made me think a bit, that story that
    you told.
The fig-leaf belt and Rory Bory are such odd
    extremes,
  Yet after all how very small this old world
    seems to be . . .

WHILE THE BANNOCK BAKES

Yes, that was quite a yarn, old pal, and yet to
 me it seems
 You missed the point: the point is that the
  "doctor chap" . . . was *me.*

THE LOST MASTER

" AND when I come to die," he said,
  " Ye shall not lay me out in state,
Nor leave your laurels at my head,
  Nor cause your men of speech orate;
No monument your gift shall be,
  No column in the Hall of Fame;
But just this line ye grave for me:
    ' He played the game.' "

So when his glorious task was done,
  It was not of his fame we thought;
It was not of his battles won,
  But of the pride with which he fought;
But of his zest, his ringing laugh,
  His trenchant scorn of praise or blame:
And so we graved his epitaph,
    " He played the game."

THE LOST MASTER

And so we, too, in humbler ways
  Went forth to fight the fight anew,
And heeding neither blame nor praise,
  We held the course he set us true.
And we, too, find the fighting sweet;
  And we, too, fight for fighting's sake;
And though we go down in defeat,
  And though our stormy hearts may break,
We will not do our Master shame:
We'll play the game, please God,
    We'll play the game.

LITTLE MOCCASINS

Come out, O Little Moccasins, and frolic on the
    snow!
  Come out, O tiny beaded feet, and twinkle in
    the light!
I'll play the old Red River reel, you used to love
    it so:
  Awake, O Little Moccasins, and dance for me
    to-night!

Your hair was all a gleamy gold, your eyes a
    corn-flower blue;
  Your cheeks were pink as tinted shells, you
    stepped light as a fawn;
Your mouth was like a coral bud, with seed
    pearls peeping through;
  As gladdening as Spring you were, as radiant
    as dawn.

LITTLE MOCCASINS

Come out, O Little Moccasins! I'll play so soft
    and low,
  The songs you loved, the old heart-songs that
    in my mem'ry ring;
O child, I want to hear you now beside the camp-
    fire glow!
  With all your heart a-throbbing in the simple
    words you sing.

For there was only you and I, and you were all
    to me;
  And round us were the barren lands, but little
    did we fear;
Of all God's happy, happy folks the happiest
    were we . . .
  (Oh, call her, poor old fiddle mine, and maybe
    she will hear!)

Your mother was a half-breed Cree, but you
    were white all through;
  And I your father was—but, well, that's
    neither here nor there;
I only know, my little Queen, that all my world
    was you,
  And now that world can end to-night, and I
    will never care.

LITTLE MOCCASINS

For there's a tiny wooden cross that pricks up
    through the snow:
  (Poor Little Moccasins! you're tired, and so
    you lie at rest.)
And there's a grey-haired, weary man beside the
    camp-fire glow:
  (O fiddle mine! the tears to-night are drum-
    ming on your breast.)

THE WANDERLUST

THE Wanderlust has lured me to the seven
     lonely seas,
  Has dumped me on the tailing-piles of dearth;
The Wanderlust has haled me from the morris
     chairs of ease,
  Has hurled me to the ends of all the earth.
How bitterly I've cursed it, oh, the Painted
     Desert knows,
  The wraithlike heights that hug the pallid
     plain,
The all-but-fluid silence—yet the longing grows
     and grows,
  And I've got to glut the Wanderlust again.

    Soldier, sailor, in what a plight I've been!
    Tinker, tailor, oh, what a sight I've seen!
    And I'm hitting the trail in the morning,
      boys,
      And you won't see my heels for dust;
     For it's " all day " with you
     When you answer the cue
      Of the Wan-der-lust.

THE WANDERLUST

The Wanderlust has got me . . . **by the**
    belly-aching fire,
  By the fever and the freezing and the pain;
By the darkness that just drowns you, by **the**
    wail of home desire,
  I've tried to break the spell of it—in vain.
Life might have been a feast for me, now there
    are only crumbs;
  In rags and tatters, beggar-wise I sit;
Yet there's no rest or peace for me, imperious **it**
    drums,
  The Wanderlust, and I must follow it.

    Highway, by-way, many a mile I've done;
    Rare way, fair way, many a height I've
      won;
    But I'm pulling my freight in the **morning,**
      boys,
      And it's over the hills or bust;
    For there's never a cure
    When you list to the lure
      Of the Wan-der-lust.

The Wanderlust has taught me . . . **it has**
    whispered to my heart
Things all you stay-at-homes will **never know.**

THE WANDERLUST

The white man and the savage are but three
      short days apart,
  Three days of cursing, crawling, doubt and
      woe.
Then it's down to chewing muclucs, to the water
      you can *eat*,
  To fish you bolt with nose held in your hand.
When you get right down to cases, it's King
      Grub that rules the races,
  And the Wanderlust will help you understand.

    Haunting, taunting, that is the spell of it;
    Mocking, baulking, that is the hell of it;
    But I'll shoulder my pack in the morning,
        boys,
      And I'm going because I must;
     For it's so-long to all
     When you answer the call
       Of the Wan-der-lust.

The Wanderlust has blest me . . . in a
      ragged blanket curled,
  I've watched the gulf of Heaven foam with
      stars;
I've walked with eyes wide open to the wonder
      of the world,
  I've seen God's flood of glory burst its bars.

THE WANDERLUST

I've seen the gold a-blinding in the riffles of the
sky,
  Till I fancied me a bloated plutocrat;
But I'm freedom's happy bond-slave, and I will
be till I die,
  And I've got to thank the Wanderlust for that.

  Wild heart, child heart, all of the world
      your home.
  Glad heart, mad heart, what can you do but
      roam?
  Oh, I'll beat it once more in the morning,
      boys,
    With a pinch of tea and a crust;
  For you cannot deny
  When you hark to the cry
    Of the Wan-der-lust.

The Wanderlust will claim me at the finish for
its own.
  I'll turn my back on men and face the Pole.
Beyond the Arctic outposts I will venture all
alone;
  Some Never-never Land will be my goal.
Thank God! there's none will miss me, for I've
been a bird of flight;

THE WANDERLUST

And in my moccasins I'll take my call;
  For the Wanderlust has ruled me,
  And the Wanderlust has schooled me,
And I'm ready for the darkest trail of all.

    Grim land, dim land, oh, how the vastness
      calls!
    Far land, star land, oh, how the stillness
      falls!
    For you never can tell if it's heaven or hell,
      And I'm taking the trail on trust;
     But I haven't a doubt
     That my soul will leap out
      On its Wan-der-lust.

THE TRAPPER'S CHRISTMAS EVE

IT'S mighty lonesome-like and drear.
  Above the Wild the moon rides high,
And shows up sharp and needle-clear
  The emptiness of earth and sky;
No happy homes with love aglow;
  No Santa Claus to make believe:
Just snow and snow, and then more snow;
  It's Christmas Eve, it's Christmas Eve.

And here am I where all things end,
  And Undesirables are hurled;
A poor old man without a friend,
  Forgot and dead to all the world;
Clean out of sight and out of mind. . . .
  Well, maybe it is better so;
We all in life our level find,
  And mine, I guess, is pretty low.

THE TRAPPER'S CHRISTMAS EVE

Yet as I sit with pipe alight
  Beside the cabin-fire, it's queer
This mind of mine must take to-night
  The backward trail of fifty year.
The school-house and the Christmas tree;
  The children with their cheeks aglow;
Two bright blue eyes that smile on me . . .
  Just half a century ago.

Again (it's maybe forty years),
  With faith and trust almost divine,
These same blue eyes, abrim with tears,
  Through depths of love look into mine.
A parting, tender, soft and low,
  With arms that cling and lips that cleave—
Ah me! it's all so long ago,
  Yet seems so sweet this Christmas Eve.

Just thirty years ago again . . .
  We say a bitter, *last* good-bye;
Our lips are white with wrath and pain;
  Our little children cling and cry.
Whose was the fault? It matters not,
  For man and woman both deceive;
It's buried now and all forgot,
  Forgiven, too, this Christmas Eve.

THE TRAPPER'S CHRISTMAS EVE

And she (God pity me) is dead;
   Our children men and women grown.
I like to think that they are wed,
   With little children of their own,
That crowd around their Christmas tree . . .
   I would not ever have them grieve,
Nor shed a single tear for me,
   To mar their joy this Christmas Eve.

Stripped to the buff and gaunt and still
   Lies all the land in grim distress.
Like lost soul wailing, long and shrill,
   A wolf-howl cleaves the emptiness.
Then hushed as Death is everything.
   The moon rides haggard and forlorn . . .
" O hark the herald angels sing!"
   God bless all men—it's Christmas morn.

THE WORLD'S ALL RIGHT

Be honest, kindly, simple, true;
Seek good in all, scorn but pretence;
Whatever sorrow come to you,
Believe in Life's Beneficence!

The World's all right; serene I sit,
And cease to puzzle over it.
There's much that's mighty strange, no doubt;
But Nature knows what she's about;
And in a million years or so
We'll know more than to-day we know.
Old Evolution's under way—
    What ho! the World's all right, I say.

Could things be other than they are?
All's in its place, from mote to star.
The thistledown that flits and flies
Could drift no hairsbreadth otherwise.
What is, must be; with rhythmic laws
All Nature chimes, Effect and Cause.
The sand-grain and the sun obey—
    What ho! the World's all right, I say.

THE WORLD'S ALL RIGHT

Just try to get the Cosmic touch,
The sense that " you " don't matter much.
A million stars are in the sky;
A million planets plunge and die.
A million million men are sped;
A million million wait ahead.
Each plays his part and has his day—
    What ho! the World's all right, I say.

Just try to get the Chemic view:
A million million lives made " you."
In lives a million you will be
Immortal down Eternity;
Immortal on this earth to range,
With never death, but ever change.
You always were, and will be aye—
    What ho! the World's all right, I say.

Be glad! And do not blindly grope
For Truth that lies beyond our scope:
A sober plot informeth all
Of Life's uproarious carnival.
Your day is such a little one,
A gnat that lives from sun to sun;
Yet gnat and you have parts to play—
    What ho! the World's all right, I say.

THE WORLD'S ALL RIGHT

And though it's written from the start,
Just act your best your little part.
Just be as happy as you can,
And serve your kind, and die—a man.
Just live the good that in you lies,
And seek no guerdon of the skies;
Just make your Heaven here, to-day—
    What ho! the World's all right, I say.

Remember! in Creation's swing
The Race and not the man's the thing.
There's battle, murder, sudden death,
And pestilence, with poisoned breath.
Yet quick forgotten are such woes;
On, on the stream of Being flows.
Truth, Beauty, Love maintain their sway—
    What ho! the World's all right, I say.

The World's all right; serene I sit,
And joy that I am part of it;
And put my trust in Nature's plan,
And try to aid her all I can;
Content to pass, if in my place
I've served the uplift of the Race.
Truth! Beauty! Love! O Radiant Day—
    What ho! the World's all right, I say.

THE BALDNESS OF CHEWED-EAR

WHEN Chewed-ear Jenkins got hitched up to
      Guinneyveer McGee,
His flowin' locks, ye recollect, wuz frivolous an'
      free;
But in old Hymen's jack-pot, it's a most amazin'
      thing,
Them flowin' locks jest disappeared like snow-
      balls in the Spring;
Jest seemed to wilt an' fade away like dead
      leaves in the Fall,
An' left old Chewed-ear balder than a white-
      washed cannon ball.

Now Missis Chewed-ear Jenkins, that wuz Guin-
      neyveer McGee,
  Wuz jest about as fine a draw as ever made a
      pair;
But when the boys got joshin' an' suggested it
      was she
  That must be inflooenshul for the old man's
      slump in hair—
  Why! Missis Chewed-ear Jenkins jest went
      clean up in the air.

THE BALDNESS OF CHEWED-EAR

" To demonstrate," sez she that night, " the
      lovin' wife I am,
I've bought a dozen bottles of Bink's Anty-Dan-
      druff Balm.
'Twill make yer hair jest sprout an' curl like
      squash-vines in the sun,
An' I propose to sling it on till every drop is
      done."
That hit old Chewed-ear's funny side, so he lays
      back an' hollers:
" The day you raise a hair, old girl, you'll git a
      thousand dollars."

Now, whether 'twas the prize or not 'tis mighty
      hard to say,
But Chewed-ear didn't seem to have much com-
      fort from that day.
With bottles of that dandruff dope she followed
      at his heels,
An' sprinkled an' massaged him even when he
      ate his meals.
She waked him from his beauty sleep with ten-
      der, lovin' care,
An' rubbed an' scrubbed assiduous, yet never
      sign of hair.

THE BALDNESS OF CHEWED-EAR

Well, naturally all the boys soon tumbled to the
joke,
An' at the Wow-wow's Social 'twas Cold-deck
Davis spoke:
" The little woman's workin' mighty hard on
Chewed-ear's crown;
Let's give her for a three-fifth's share a hundred
dollars down.
We stand to make five hundred clear—boys,
drink in whiskey straight:
' The Chewed-ear Jenkins Hirsute Propagation
Syndicate.' "

The boys wuz on, an' soon chipped in the neces-
sary dust;
They primed up a committy to negotiate the
deal;
Then Missis Jenkins yielded, bein' rather in dis-
gust,
An' all wuz signed an' witnessed, an' invested
with a seal.
They rounded up old Chewed-ear, an' they broke
it what they'd done;
Allowed they'd bought an interest in his
chance of raisin' hair;

THE BALDNESS OF CHEWED-EAR

They yanked his hat off anxious-like, opinin' one
    by one,
  Their magnifyin'-glasses showed fine pro-
    spects everywhere.
They bought Hairlene, an' Thatchem, an' Jay's
    Cappillery Juice,
  An' Seven Something Sisters, an' Macassar
    an' Bay Rum,
An' everyone insisted on his speshul right to
    sluice
  His speshul line of lotion onto Chewed-ear's
    cranium.
They only got the merrier the more the old man
    roared,
An' shares in " Jenkins Hirsute " went sky-
    highin' on the board.

The Syndicate wuz hopeful that they'd demon-
    strate the pay,
An' Missis Jenkins labored in her perseverin'
    way.
The boys discussed on " surface rights," an'
    " out-crops," an' so on,
An' planned to have it " crown " surveyed, an'
    blueprints of it drawn.

THE BALDNESS OF CHEWED-EAR

They ran a base line, sluiced an' yelled, an'
    everyone wuz glad,
Except the balance of the property, an' he wuz
    " mad."
" It gives me pain," he interjects, " to squash
    yer glowin' dream,
But you wuz fools when you got in on this here
    ' Hirsute ' scheme.
You'll never raise a hair on me "—when lo! that
    very night,
Preparin' to retire, he got a most onpleasant
    fright:
For on that shinin' dome of his, so prominently
    bare,
He felt the baby outcrop of a second growth of
    hair.

A thousand dollars! Sufferin' Cæsar! Well, it
    must be saved!
He grabbed his razor recklesslike, an' shaved an'
    shaved an' shaved.
An' when his head wuz smooth again he gives a
    mighty sigh,
An' sneaks away, an' buys some Hair Destroyer
    on the sly.

THE BALDNESS OF CHEWED-EAR

So there wuz Missis Jenkins with " **Restorer** "
    wagin' fight,
An' Chewed-ear with " Destroyer " **circum-**
    ventin' her at night.
The battle wuz a mighty one; his nerves wuz on
    the strain,
An' yet in spite of all he did that hair began to
    gain.

The situation grew intense, so quietly one day,
He gave his shareholders the slip, an' made his
    get-away.
Jest like a criminal he skipped, an' aimed to
    defalcate
The Chewed-ear Jenkins Hirsute Propagation
    Syndicate.
His guilty secret burned him, an' he sought the
    city's din:
" I've got to get a wig," sez he, " to cover up my
    sin.
It's growin', growin', night an' day; it's most
    amazin' hair;"
An' when he looked at it that night, he shud-
    dered with despair.
He shuddered an' suppressed a cry at what his
    optics seen—
For on my word of honour, boys, that hair wuz
    growin' *green*.

THE BALDNESS OF CHEWED-EAR

At first he guessed he'd get some dye, an' try to
      dye it black;
An' then he saw 'twas Nemmysis wuz layin' on
      his track.
He must jest face the music, an' confess the
      thing he'd done,
An' pay the boys an' Guinneyveer the money they
      had won.
An' then there came a big idee—it thrilled him
      like a shock:
Why not control the Syndicate by buyin' up the
      stock?

An' so next day he hurried back with smoothly
      shaven pate,
An' for a hundred dollars he bought up the Syn-
      dicate.
'Twas mighty frenzied finance an' the boys set
      up a roar,
But "Hirsutes" from the market wuz with-
      drawn for evermore.
An' to this day in Nuggetsville they tell the tale
      how slick
The Syndicate sold out too soon, and Chewed-
      ear turned the trick.

THE MOTHER

THERE will be a singing in your heart,
  There will be a rapture in your eyes;
You will be a woman set apart,
  You will be so wonderful and wise.
You will sleep, and when from dreams you start,
  As of one that wakes in Paradise,
There will be a singing in your heart,
  There will be a rapture in your eyes.

There will be a moaning in your heart,
  There will be an anguish in your eyes;
You will see your dearest ones depart,
  You will hear their quivering good-byes.
Yours will be the heart-ache and the smart,
  Tears that scald and lonely sacrifice;
There will be a moaning in your heart,
  There will be an anguish in your eyes.

THE MOTHER

There will come a glory in your eyes,
    There will come a peace within your heart;
Sitting 'neath the quiet evening skies,
    Time will dry the tear and dull the smart.
You will know that you have played your part;
    Yours shall be the love that never dies:
You, with Heaven's peace within your heart,
    You, with God's own glory in your eyes.

THE DREAMER

THE lone man gazed and gazed upon his gold,
  His sweat, his blood, the wage of weary days;
But now how sweet, how doubly sweet to hold
  All gay and gleamy to the camp-fire blaze.
The evening sky was sinister and cold;
  The willows shivered, wanly lay the snow;
The uncommiserating land, so old,
  So worn, so grey, so niggard in its woe,
Peered through its ragged shroud.   The lone
      man sighed,
  Poured back the gaudy dust into its poke,
Gazed at the seething river listless-eyed,
  Loaded his corn-cob pipe as if to smoke;
Then crushed with weariness and hardship
      crept
Into his ragged robe, and swiftly slept.

  .   .   .   .

Hour after hour went by; a shadow slipped
  From vasts of shadow to the camp-fire flame;
  Gripping a rifle with a deadly aim,
A gaunt and hairy man with wolfish eyes. . . .

  *   *   *   *   *   *   *   *

THE DREAMER

The sleeper dreamed, and lo! this was his dream:
  He rode a streaming horse across a moor.
Sudden 'mid pit-black night a lightning gleam
  Showed him a wayside inn, forlorn and poor.
A sullen host unbarred the creaking door,
  And led him to a dim and dreary room,
Wherein he sat and poked the fire a-roar,
  So that weird shadows jigged athwart the
     gloom.
He ordered wine. 'Od's blood! but he was tired.
  What matter! Charles was crushed and
     George was King;
His party high in power; how he aspired!
  Red guineas packed his purse, too tight to
     ring.
The firelight gleamed upon his silken hose,
  His silver buckles and his powdered wig.
What ho! more wine! He drank, he slowly rose.
  What made the shadows dance that madcap
     jig?
He clutched the candle, steered his way to bed,
And in a trice was sleeping like the dead.

    .   .   .   .

Across the room there crept, so shadow soft,
  His sullen host, with naked knife agleam,
(A gaunt and hairy man with wolfish eyes.) . . .
  And as he lay, the sleeper dreamed a dream:

  *   *   *   *   *   *   *   *

THE DREAMER

'Twas in a ruder land, a wilder day.
  A rival princeling sat upon his throne,
Within a dungeon dark and foul he lay,
  With chains that bit and festered to the bone.
They haled him harshly to a vaulted room,
  Where One gazed on him with malignant eye;
And in that devil-face he read his doom,
  Knowing that ere the dawn-light he must die.
Well, he was sorrow-glutted; let them bring
  Their prize assassins to the bloody work.
His kingdom lost, yet would he die a King,
  Peerless and proud, as when he faced the
    Turk.
Ah, God! the glory of that great Crusade!
  The bannered pomp, the gleam, the splendid
    urge!
The crash of reeking combat, blade to blade!
  The reeling ranks, blood-avid and a-surge!
For long he thought; then feeling o'er him creep
Vast weariness, he fell into a sleep.

    .   .   .   .

The cell door opened; soft the headsman came,
  Within his hand a mighty axe agleam,
(A gaunt and hairy man with wolfish eyes.) . . .
  And as he lay, the sleeper dreamed a dream:

  *   *   *   *   *   *   *   *

THE DREAMER

'Twas in a land unkempt, of life's red dawn,
   Where in his sanded cave he dwelt alone;
Sleeping by day, or sometimes worked upon
   His flint-head arrows and his knives of stone;
By night stole forth and slew the savage boar,
   So that he loomed a hunter of loud fame,
And many a skin of wolf and wild-cat wore,
   And counted many a flint-head to his name;
Wherefore he walked the envy of the band,
   Hated and feared, but matchless in his skill.
Till lo! one night deep in that shaggy land,
   He tracked a yearling bear and made his kill;
Then over-worn he rested by a stream,
And sank into a sleep too deep for dream.

    .   .   .   .

Hunting his food a rival caveman crept
   Through those dark woods, and marked him
      where he lay;
Cowered and crawled upon him as he slept,
   Poising a mighty stone aloft to slay—
(A gaunt and hairy man with wolfish eyes.) . . .

   *   *   *   *   *   *   *   *

The great stone crashed. The Dreamer shrieked
      and woke,
   And saw, fear-blinded, in his dripping cell,

THE DREAMER

A gaunt and hairy man, who with one stroke
    Swung a great axe of steel that flashed and
        fell. . . .

So that he woke amid his bed-room gloom,
    And saw, hair-poised, a naked, thirsting knife,
A gaunt and hairy man with eyes of doom—
    And then the blade plunged down to drink his
        life. . . .

So that he woke, wrenched back his robe, and
        looked,
    And saw beside his dying fire upstart
A gaunt and hairy man with finger crooked—
    A rifle rang, a bullet searched his heart. . . .

*   *   *   *   *   *   *   *

The morning sky was sinister and cold.
    Grotesque the Dreamer sprawled, and did not
        rise.
For long and long there gazed upon some gold
    A gaunt and hairy man with wolfish eyes.

AT THIRTY-FIVE

THREE score and ten, the Psalmist saith,
  And half my course is well nigh run;
I've had my flout at dusty death,
  I've had my whack of feast and fun.
I've mocked at those who prate and preach;
  I've laughed with any man alive;
But now with sobered heart I reach
  The Great Divide of Thirty-five.

And looking back I must confess
  I've little cause to feel elate.
I've played the mummer more or less;
  I fumbled fortune, flouted fate.
I've vastly dreamed and little done;
  I've idly watched my brothers strive:
Oh, I have loitered in the sun
  By primrose paths to Thirty-five!

AT THIRTY-FIVE

And those who matched me in the race,
  Well, some are out and trampled down;
The others jog with sober pace;
  Yet one wins delicate renown.
O midnight feast and famished dawn!
  O gay, hard life, with hope alive!
O golden youth, forever gone,
  How sweet you seem at Thirty-five!

Each of our lives is just a book
  As absolute as Holy Writ;
We humbly read, and may not look
  Ahead, nor change one word of it.
And here are joys and here are pains;
  And here we fail and here we thrive;
O wondrous volume! What remains
  When we reach chapter Thirty-five?

The very best, I dare to hope,
  Ere Fate writes Finis to the tome;
A wiser head, a wider scope,
  And for the gipsy heart, a home;
A songful home, with loved ones near,
  With joy, with sunshine all alive:
Watch me grow younger every year—
  Old Age! thy name is Thirty-five!

THE SQUAW-MAN

THE cow-moose comes to water, and the beaver's
    overbold,
  The net is in the eddy of the stream;
The tepee stars the vivid sward with russet, red
    and gold,
  And in the velvet gloom the fire's agleam.
The night is ripe with quiet, rich with incense
    of the pine;
  From sanctuary lake I hear the loon;
The peaks are bright against the blue, and
    drenched with sunset wine,
  And like a silver bubble is the moon.

Cloud-high I climbed but yesterday; a hundred
    miles around
  I looked to see a rival fire agleam.
As in a crystal lens it lay, a land without a
    bound,
  All lure, and virgin vastitude, and dream.

THE SQUAW-MAN

The great sky roared exultantly, the great earth
     bared its breast,
  All river-veined and patterned with the pine;
The heedless hordes of caribou were streaming
     to the West,
  A land of lustrous mystery—and mine.

Yea, mine to frame my Odyssey: Oh, little do
     they know
  My conquest and the kingdom that I keep!
The meadows of the musk-ox where the laugh-
     ing grasses grow,
  The rivers where the careless conies leap.
Beyond the silent Circle, where white men are
     fierce and few,
  I lord it, and I mock at man-made law;
Like a flame upon the water is my little light
     canoe,
  And yonder in the fireglow is my squaw.

A squaw-man! yes that's what I am; sneer at
     me if you will.
  I've gone the grilling pace that cannot last;
With bawdry, bridge and brandy—Oh, I've
     drunk enough to kill
  A dozen such as you, but that is past.

THE SQUAW-MAN

I've swung round to my senses, found the place
　　where I belong;
　The City made a madman out of me;
But here beyond the Circle, where there's neither
　　right or wrong,
　I leap from life's straight-jacket, and I'm free.

Yet ever in the far forlorn, by trails of lone
　　desire;
　Yet ever in the dawn's white leer of hate;
Yet ever by the dripping kill, beside the drowsy
　　fire,
　　There comes the fierce heart-hunger for a
　　　mate.
There comes the mad blood-clamour for a
　　woman's clinging hand,
　Love-humid eyes, the velvet of a breast:
And so I sought the Bonnet-plumes, and chose
　　from out the band
　　The girl I thought the sweetest and the best.

O wistful women I have loved before my dark
　　disgrace!
　O women fair and rare in my home land!

THE SQUAW-MAN

Dear ladies, if I saw you now I'd turn away my
      face,
  Then crawl to kiss your foot-prints in the
      sand!
And yet—that day the rifle jammed—a wounded
      moose at bay—
  A roar, a charge .   .   . I faced it with my
      knife:
A shot from out the willow-scrub, and there the
      monster lay .   .   .
  Yes, little Laughing Eyes, you saved my life.

The man must have the woman, and we're all
      brutes more or less,
  Since first the male ape shinned the family
      tree;
And yet I think I love her with a husband's ten-
      derness,
  And yet I know that she would die for me.
Oh, if I left you, Laughing Eyes, and nevermore
      came back,
  God help you, girl! I know what you would
      do .   .   .
I see the lake wan in the moon, and from the
      shadow black,
  There drifts a little *empty* birch canoe.

THE SQUAW-MAN

We're here beyond the Circle, where there's never
     wrong nor right;
  We aren't spliced according to the law;
But by the gods I hail you on this hushed and
     holy night
  As the mother of my children, and my squaw.
I see your little slender face set in the firelight
     glow;
  I pray that I may never make it sad;
I hear you croon a baby song, all slumber-soft
     and low—
  God bless you, little Laughing Eyes! I'm glad.

HOME AND LOVE

Just Home and Love! the words are small,
  Four little letters unto each;
And yet you will not find in all
  The wide and gracious range of speech
Two more so tenderly complete:
  When angels talk in Heaven above,
I'm sure they have no words more sweet
    Than Home and Love.

Just Home and Love! it's hard to guess
  Which of the two were best to gain;
Home without Love is bitterness;
  Love without Home is often pain.
No! each alone will seldom do;
  Somehow they travel hand and glove:
If you win one you must have two,
    Both Home and Love.

HOME AND LOVE

And if you've both, well, then I'm sure
   You ought to sing the whole day long;
It doesn't matter if you're poor
   With these to make divine your song.
And so I praisefully repeat,
   When angels talk in Heaven above,
There are no words more simply sweet
   Than Home and Love.

I'M SCARED OF IT ALL

I'M scared of it all, God's truth! so I am;
   It's too big and brutal for me.
My nerve's on the raw and I don't give a damn
   For all the " hoorah " that I see.
I'm pinned between subway and overhead train,
   Where automobillies swoop down:
Oh, I want to go back to the timber again—
   I'm scared of the terrible town.

I want to go back to my lean, ashen plains;
   My rivers that flash into foam:
My ultimate valleys where solitude reigns;
   My trail from Fort Churchill to Nome.
My forests packed full of mysterious gloom,
   My ice-fields agrind and aglare:
The city is deadfalled with danger and doom—
   I know that I'm safer up there.

I'M SCARED OF IT ALL

I watcn tne wan faces that flash in the street;
   All kinds and all classes I see.
Yet never a one in the million I meet
   Has the smile of a comrade for me.
Just jaded and panting like dogs in a pack;
   Just tensed and intent on the goal:
O God! but I'm lonesome—I wish I was back,
   Up there in the land of the Pole.

I wish I was back on the Hunger Plateaus,
   And seeking the lost caribou;
I wish I was up where the Coppermine flows
   To the kick of my little canoe.
I'd like to be far on some weariful shore,
   In the Land of the Blizzard and Bear;
Oh, I wish I was snug in the Arctic once more,
   For I know I am safer up there!

I prowl in the canyons of dismal unrest;
   I cringe—I'm so weak and so small.
I can't get my bearings, I'm crushed and
      oppressed
   With the haste and the waste of it all.

I'M SCARED OF IT ALL

The slaves and the madmen, the lust and the
    sweat,
  The fear in the faces I see;
The getting, the spending, the fever, the fret—
  It's too bleeding cruel for me.

I feel it's all wrong, but I can't tell you why—
  The palace, the hovel next door;
The insolent towers that sprawl to the sky,
  The crush and the rush and the roar.
I'm trapped like a fox and I fear for my pelt;
  I cower in the crash and the glare;
Oh, I want to be back in the avalanche belt,
  For I know that it's safer up there!

I'm scared of it all. Oh, afar I can hear
  The voice of my solitudes call!
We're nothing but brute with a little veneer,
  And nature is best after all.
There's tumult and terror abroad in the street;
  There's menace and doom in the air;
I've got to get back to my thousand-mile beat;
The trail where the cougar and silver-tip meet;
The snows and the camp-fire, with wolves at my
    feet;
  Good-bye, for it's safer up there.

I'M SCARED OF IT ALL

To be forming good habits up there;
To be starving on rabbits up there;
In your hunger and woe,
Though it's sixty below,
Oh, I know that it's safer up there!

A SONG OF SUCCESS

Ho! we were strong, we were swift, we were
     brave.
  Youth was a challenge, and Life was a fight.
All that was best in us gladly we gave,
  Sprang from the rally, and leapt for the height.
Smiling is Love in a foam of Spring flowers:
  Harden our hearts to him—on let us press!
Oh, what a triumph and pride shall be ours!
  See where it beacons, the star of success!

Cares seem to crowd on us—so much to do;
  New fields to conquer, and time's on the wing.
Grey hairs are showing, a wrinkle or two;
  Somehow our footstep is losing its spring.
Pleasure's forsaken us, Love ceased to smile;
  Youth has been funeralled; Age travels fast.
Sometimes we wonder: Is it worth while?
  There! we have gained to the summit at last.

A SONG OF SUCCESS

Aye, we have triumphed! Now must we haste,
  Revel in victory . . . why! what is wrong?
Life's choicest vintage is flat to the taste—
  Are we too late? Have we laboured too long?
Wealth, power, fame we hold . . . ah! but
        the truth:
  Would we not give this vain glory of ours
For one mad, glad year of glorious youth,
  Life in the Springtide, and Love in the flowers?

THE SONG OF THE CAMP-FIRE

I.

HEED me, feed me, I am hungry, I am red-
tongued with desire;
  Boughs of balsam, slabs of cedar, gummy fag-
gots of the pine,
Heap them on me, let me hug them to my eager
heart of fire,
  Roaring, soaring up to heaven as a symbol and
a sign.
Bring me knots of sunny maple, silver birch and
tamarack;
  Leaping, sweeping, I will lap them with my
ardent wings of flame;
I will kindle them to glory, I will beat the darkness back;
  Streaming, gleaming, I will goad them to my
glory and my fame.
Bring me gnarly limbs of live-oak, aid me in my
frenzied fight;
  Strips of iron-wood, scaly blue-gum, writhing
redly in my hold;

THE SONG OF THE CAMP-FIRE

With my lunge of lurid lances, with my whips
    that flail the night,
  They will burgeon into beauty, they will foli-
    ate in gold.
Let me star the dim sierras, stab with light the
    inland seas;
  Roaming wind and roaring darkness! seek
    no mercy at my hands;
I will mock the marly heavens, lamp the purple
    prairies,
  I will flaunt my deathless banners down the
    far, unhouseled lands.
In the vast and vaulted pine-gloom where the
    pillared forests frown,
  By the sullen, brutish rivers running where
    God only knows,
On the starlit coral beaches when the combers
    thunder down,
  In the death-spell of the barrens, in the shud-
    der of the snows;
In a blazing belt of triumph from the palm-leaf
    to the pine,
  As a symbol of defiance, lo! the wilderness I
    span;
And my beacons burnt exultant as an everlast-
    ing sign
  Of unending domination, of the mastery of
    Man;

THE SONG OF THE CAMP-FIRE

I, the Life, the fierce Uplifter, I that weaned him
    from the mire;
  I, the angel and the devil; I, the tyrant and
    the slave;
I, the Spirit of the Struggle; I, the mighty God
    of Fire;
  I, the Maker and Destroyer; I, the Giver and
    the Grave.

II.

Gather round me, boy and grey-beard, frontiers-
    men of every kind.
Few are you, and far and lonely, yet an army
    forms behind:
By your camp-fires shall they know you, ashes
    scattered to the wind.

Peer into my heart of solace, break your ban-
    nock at my blaze;
Smoking, stretched in lazy shelter, build **your**
    castles as you gaze;
Or, it may be, deep in dreaming, think of **dim,**
    unhappy days.

THE SONG OF THE CAMP-FIRE

Let my warmth and glow caress you, for your
    trails are grim and hard;
Let my arms of comfort press you, hunger-hewn
    and battle-scarred:
O my lovers! how I bless you with your lives so
    madly marred!

For you seek the silent spaces, and their secret
    lore you glean;
For you win the savage races, and the brutish
    Wild you wean;
And I gladden desert places, where camp-fire has
    never been.

From the Pole unto the Tropics is there trail
    ye have not dared?
And because you hold death lightly, so by death
    shall you be spared,
(As the sages of the ages in their pages have
    declared.)

On the roaring Arkilinik in a leaky bark canoe;
Up the cloud of Mount McKinley, where the
    avalanche leaps through;
In the furnace of Death Valley, when the mirage
    glimmers blue.

THE SONG OF THE CAMP-FIRE

Now a smudge of wiry willows on the weary
      Kuskoquim;
Now a flare of gummy pine-knots where Van-
      couver's scaur is grim;
Now a gleam of sunny ceiba, when the Cuban
      beaches dim.

Always, always God's Great Open: lo! I burn
      with keener light
In the corridors of silence, in the vestibules of
      night;
'Mid the ferns and grasses gleaming, was there
      ever gem so bright?

Not for weaklings, not for women, like my
      brother of the hearth;
Ring your songs of wrath around me, I was
      made for manful mirth,
In the lusty, gusty greatness, on the bald spots
      of the earth.

Men, my masters! Men, my lovers! ye have
      fought and ye have bled;
Gather round my ruddy embers, softly glowing
      is my bed;
By my heart of solace dreaming, rest ye and be
      comforted!

THE SONG OF THE CAMP-FIRE

III.

I am dying, O my masters! by my fitful flame ye
    sleep;
  My purple plumes of glory droop forlorn.
Grey ashes choke and cloak me, and above the
    pines there creep
  The stealthy silver moccasins of morn.
There comes a countless army, it's the Legion of
    the Light;
    It tramps in gleaming triumph round the
    world;
And before its jewelled lances all the shadows
    of the night
  Back in to abysmal darknesses are hurled.

Leap to life again, my lovers! ye must toil and
    never tire;
  The day of daring, doing, brightens clear,
When the bed of spicy cedar and the jovial camp-
    fire
  Must only be a memory of cheer.
There is hope and golden promise in the vast,
    portentous dawn;
  There is glamour in the glad, effluent sky:
Go and leave me; I will dream of you and love
    you when you're gone;
  I have served you, O my masters! let me die.

THE SONG OF THE CAMP-FIRE

A little heap of ashes, grey and sodden by the
     rain,
  Wind-scattered, blurred and blotted by the
     snow:
Let that be all to tell of me, and glorious again,
  Ye things of greening gladness, leap and glow!
A black scar in the sunshine by the palm-leaf
     or the pine,
  Blind to the night and dead to all desire;
Yet oh, of life and uplift what a symbol and a
     sign!
Yet oh, of power and conquest what a destiny is
     mine!
A little heap of ashes—Yea! a miracle divine,
  The foot-print of a god, all-radiant Fire.

HER LETTER

" I'M taking pen in hand this night, and hard it
     is for me;
   My poor old fingers tremble so, my hand is
     stiff and slow,
And even with my glasses on I'm troubled sore
     to see . . .
   You'd little know your mother, boy; you'd
     little, little know.
You mind how brisk and bright I was, how
     straight and trim and smart;
   'Tis weariful I am the now, and bent and
     frail and grey.
I'm waiting at the road's end, lad; and all
    '   that's in my heart,
   Is just to see my boy again before I'm called
     away.

HER LETTER

" Oh, well I mind the sorry day you crossed the
    gurly sea;
    'Twas like the heart was torn from me, a
    waeful wife was I.
You said that you'd be home again in two
    years, maybe three;
    But nigh a score of years have gone, and
    still the years go by.
I know it's cruel hard for you, you've bairnies
    of your own;
    I know the siller's hard to win, and folks
    have used you ill:
But oh, think of your mother, lad, that's wait-
    ing by her lone!
    And even if you canna come—*just write and
    say you will.*

" Aye, even though there's little hope, just pro-
    mise that you'll try.
    It's weary, weary waiting, lad; just say
    you'll come next year.
I'm thinking there will be no ' next '; I'm
    thinking soon I'll lie
    With all the ones I've laid away . . .
    but oh, the hope will cheer.'

HER LETTER

You know you're all that's left to me, and we
    are seas apart;
  But if you'll only *say* you'll come, then will
    I hope and pray.
I'm waiting by the grave-side, lad; and all
    that's in my heart
  Is just to see my boy again before I'm called
    away."

THE MAN WHO KNEW

THE Dreamer visioned Life as it might be,
  And from his dream forthright a picture grew,
A painting all the people thronged to see,
  And joyed therein—till came the Man Who
      Knew,
Saying: " 'Tis bad! Why do ye gape, ye fools?
He painteth not according to the schools."

The Dreamer probed Life's mystery of woe,
  And in a book he sought to give the clue;
The people read, and saw that it was so,
  And read again—then came the Man Who
      Knew,
Saying: " Ye witless ones! this book is vile:
It hath not got the rudiments of style."

THE MAN WHO KNEW

Love smote the Dreamer's lips, and silver-clear
  He sang a song so sweet, so tender true,
That all the market-place was thrilled to hear,
  And listened rapt—till came the Man Who
      Knew,
Saying: " His technique's wrong; he singeth ill.
Waste not your time."   The singer's voice was
      still.

And then the people roused as if from sleep,
  Crying: " What care we if it be not Art!
Hath he not charmed us, made us laugh and
      weep?
  Come, let us crown him where he sits apart."
Then, with his picture spurned, his book unread,
His song unsung, they found their **Dreamer**—
      dead.

THE LOGGER

In the moonless, misty night, with my little pipe
     alight,
  I am sitting by the camp-fire's fading cheer;
Oh, the dew is falling chill on the dim, deer-
     haunted hill,
    And the breakers in the bay are moaning
     drear.
The toilful hours are sped, the boys are long
     abed,
  And I alone a weary vigil keep;
In the sightless, sullen sky I can hear the night-
     hawk cry,
    And the frogs in frenzied chorus from the
     creek.

And somehow the ember's glow brings me back
     the long ago,
  The days of merry laughter and light song;
When I sped the hours away with the gayest of
     the gay
  In the giddy whirl of fashion's festal throng.

THE LOGGER

Oh, I ran a grilling race and I little recked the
   pace,
  For the lust of youth ran riot in my blood;
But at last I made a stand in this God-forsaken
   land
    Of the pine-tree and the mountain and the
    flood.

And now I've got to stay, with an overdraft to
   pay
  For pleasure in the past with future pain;
And I'm not the chap to whine, for if the chance
   were mine
  I know I'd choose the old life once again.
With its woman's eyes ashine, and its flood of
   golden wine;
  Its fever and its frolic and its fun;
The old life with its din, its laughter and its
   sin—
  And chuck me in the gutter when it's done.

Ah, well! it's past and gone, and the memory is
   wan,
  That conjures up each old familiar face;

THE LOGGER

And here by fortune hurled, I am dead to all the
    world,
    And I've learned to lose my pride and keep
      my place.
My ways are hard and rough, and my arms are
    strong and tough,
    And I hew the dizzy pine till darkness falls;
And sometimes I take a dive, just to keep my
    heart alive,
    Among the gay saloons and dancing-halls.

In the distant, dinful town just a little drink, to
    drown
    The cares that crowd and canker in my brain;
Just a little joy to still set my pulses all athrill,
    Then back to brutish labour once again.
And things will go on so until one day I shall
    know
    That Death has got me cinched beyond a
      doubt;
Then I'll crawl away from sight, and morosely
    in the night
    My weary, wasted life will peter out.

Then the boys will gather round, and they'll
    launch me in the ground,
    And pile on stones the timber wolf to foil;

THE LOGGER

And the moaning pine will wave overhead a
 nameless grave,
  Where the blacksnake in the sunshine loves
  to coil.
And they'll leave me there alone, and perhaps
 with softened tone
  Speak of me sometimes in the camp-fire's
  glow,
As a played-out, broken chum, who has gone to
 Kingdom Come,
  And who went the pace in England long ago.

THE PASSING OF THE YEAR

MY glass is filled, my pipe is lit,
  My den is all a cosy glow;
And snug before the fire I sit,
  And wait to *feel* the old year go.
I dedicate to solemn thought
  Amid my too-unthinking days,
This sober moment, sadly fraught
  With much of blame, with little praise.

Old Year! upon the Stage of Time
  You stand to bow your last adieu;
A moment, and the prompter's chime
  Will ring the curtain down on you.
Your mien is sad, your step is slow;
  You falter as a Sage in pain;
Yet turn, Old Year, before you go,
  And face your audience again.

179

THE PASSING OF THE YEAR

That sphynx-like face, remote, austere,
  Let us all read, whate'er the cost:
O Maiden! why that bitter tear?
  Is it for dear one you have lost?
Is it for fond illusion gone?
  For trusted lover proved untrue?
O sweet girl-face, so sad, so wan,
  What hath the Old Year meant to you?

And you, O neighbour on my right,
  So sleek, so prosperously clad!
What see you in that aged wight
  That makes your smile so gay and glad?
What opportunity unmissed?
  What golden gain, what pride of place?
What splendid hope? O Optimist!
  What read you in that withered face?

And you, deep shrinking in the gloom,
  What find you in that filmy gaze?
What menace of a tragic doom?
  What dark, condemning yesterdays?
What urge to crime, what evil done?
  What cold, confronting shape of fear?
O haggard, haunted, hidden One,
  What see you in the dying year?

THE PASSING OF THE YEAR

And so from face to face I flit,
    The countless eyes that stare and stare;
Some are with approbation lit,
    And some are shadowed with despair.
Some show a smile and some a frown;
    Some joy and hope, some pain and woe:
Enough! Oh, ring that curtain down!
    Old weary year! it's time to go.

My pipe is out, my glass is dry;
    My fire is almost ashes too;
But once again, before you go,
    And I prepare to meet the New:
Old Year! a parting word that's true,
    For we've been comrades, you and I—
I thank God for each day of you;
    There! bless you now! Old Year, good-bye!

THE GHOSTS

SMITH, great writer of stories, drank; found it
    immortalized his pen;
Fused in his brain-pan, else a blank. heavens of
    glory now and then;
Gave him the magical genius touch; God-given
    power to gouge out, fling
Flat in your face a soul-thought—Bing! Twiddle
    your heart-strings in his clutch.
"Bah!" said Smith, "let my body lie stripped
    to the buff in swinish shame,
If I can blaze in the radiant sky out of adoring
    stars my name.
Sober am I nonentitized; drunk am I more than
    half a god.
Well, let the flesh be sacrificed; spirit shall
    speak and shame the clod.
Who would not gladly, gladly give Life to do
    one thing that will live?"

THE GHOSTS

Smith had a friend, we'll call him Brown;
    dearer than brothers were those two.
When in the wassail Smith would drown, Brown
    would rescue and pull him through.
When Brown was needful Smith would lend; so
    it fell as the years went by,
Each on the other would depend: then at the
    last Smith came to die.

There Brown sat in the sick man's room, still
    as a stone in his despair;
Smith bent on him his eyes of doom. shook back
    his lion mane of hair;
Said: " Is there one in my chosen line, writer of
    forthright tales, my peer?
Look in that little desk of mine; there is a pack-
    age, bring it here.
Story of stories, gem of all; essence and triumph,
    key and clue;
Tale of a loving woman's fall; soul swept hell-
    ward, and God! it's true.
I was the man—Oh, yes, I've paid, paid with
    mighty and mordant pain.
Look! here's the masterpiece I've made out of
    my sin, my manhood slain.

THE GHOSTS

Art supreme! yet the world would stare, know
    my mistress and blaze my shame.
I have a wife and daughter—there! take it and
    thrust it in the flame."

Brown answered: " Master, you have dipped pen
    in your heart, your phrases sear.
Ruthless, unflinching, you have stripped naked
    your soul and set it here.
Have I not loved you well and true?   See!
    between us the shadows drift;
This bit of blood and tears means You—oh, let
    me have it, a parting gift.
Sacred I'll hold it, a trust divine; sacred your
    honour, her dark despair;
Never shall it see printed line: here, by the liv-
    ing God I swear."
Brown on a Bible laid his hand; Smith, great
    writer of stories, sighed:
" Comrade, I trust you, and understand. Keep
    my secret!" And so he died.

Smith was buried—upsoared his sales; lured
    you his books in every store;
Exquisite, whimsy, heart-wrung tales; men
    devoured them and craved for more.

THE GHOSTS

So when it slyly got about Brown had a post-
    humous manuscript,
Jones, the publisher, sought him out, into his
    pocket deep he dipped.
" A thousand dollars?" Brown shook his head.
    " The story is not for sale," he said.

Jones went away, then others came. Tempted
    and taunted, Brown was true.
Guarded at friendship's shrine, the fame of the
    unpublished story grew and grew.
It's a long, long lane that has no end, but some
    lanes end in the Potter's field;
Smith to Brown had been more than friend:
    patron, protector, spur and shield.
Poor, loving-wistful, dreamy Brown, long and
    lean, with a smile askew,
Friendless he wandered up and down, gaunt as
    a wolf, as hungry, too.
Brown with his lilt of saucy rhyme, Brown with
    his tilt of tender mirth,
Garretless in the gloom and grime, singing his
    glad, mad songs of earth:
So at last with a faith divine, down and down
    to the Hunger-line.

THE GHOSTS

There as he stood in a woeful plignt, tears
    a-freeze on his sharp cheek-bones,
Who should chance to behold his plight but the
    publisher, the plethoric Jones;
Peered at him for a little while, held out a bill:
    "*Now,* will you sell?"
Brown scanned it with his twisted smile: "A
    thousand dollars! you go to hell!"

Brown enrolled in the homeless host, sleeping
    anywhere, anywhen;
Suffered, strove, became a ghost, slave of the
    lamp for other men;
For What's-his-name and So-and-so in the abyss
    his soul he stripped,
Yet in his want, his worst of woe, held he fast
    to the manuscript.
Then one day as he chewed his pen, half in hun-
    ger and half despair,
Creaked the door of his garret den; Dick, his
    brother, was standing there.
Down on the pallet bed he sank, ashen his face,
    his voice a wail:
"Save me, brother! I've robbed the bank;
    to-morrow it's ruin, capture, gaol.

THE GHOSTS

Yet there's a chance: I could to-day pay back
     the money, save our name;
You have a manuscript, they say, worth a thou-
     sand—think, man! the shame . . . ."
Brown with his heart pain-pierced the while,
     with his stern, starved face, and his lips
     stone-pale,
Shuddered and smiled his twisted smile:
     " Brother, I guess you go to gaol."

While poor Brown in the leer of dawn wrestled
     with God for the sacred fire,
Came there a woman weak and wan, out of the
     mob, the murk, the mire;
Frail as a reed, a fellow ghost, weary with woe,
     with sorrowing;
Two pale souls in the legion lost; lo! Love bent
     with a tender wing,
Taught them a joy so deep, so true, it seemed
     that the whole world-fabric shook,
Thrilled and dissolved in radiant dew: then
     Brown made him a golden book,
Full of the faith that Life is good, that the earth
     is a dream divinely fair,
Lauding his gem of womanhood, in many a lyric
     rich and rare;
Took it to Jones, who shook his head: " I will
     consider it," he said.

THE GHOSTS

While he considered, Brown's wife lay clutched
    in the tentacles of pain;
Then came the doctor, grave and gray; spoke of
    decline, of nervous strain;
Hinted Egypt, the South of France—Brown
    with terror was tiger-gripped.
Where was the money? What the chance? Piti-
    ful God! . . . the manuscript!
A thousand dollars—his only hope! He gazed
    and gazed at the garret wall . . .
Reached at last for the envelope, turned to his
    wife and told her all.
Told of his friend, his promise true; told like his
    very heart would break;
" Oh, my dearest! what shall I do? Shall I not
    sell it for your sake?"
Ghostlike she lay, as still as doom; turned to
    the wall her weary head;
Icy-cold in the pallid gloom, silent as death
    . . . at last she said:
" Do, my husband! Keep your vow! Guard his
    secret and let me die . . .
Oh, my dear, I must tell you now—*the woman
    he loved and wronged was I;*
Darling! I haven't long to live: I never told
    you—forgive, forgive!"

THE GHOSTS

For a long, long time Brown did not speak; sat
    bleak-browed in the wretched room;
Slowly a tear stole down his cheek, and he kissed
    her hand in the dismal gloom.
To break his oath, to brand her shame; his well-
    loved friend, his worshipped wife;
To keep his vow, to save her name, yet at the
    cost of what? Her life!
A moment's space did he hesitate, a moment of
    pain and dread and doubt,
Then he broke the seals and, stern as fate, un-
    folded the sheets and spread them out . . .
On his knees by her side he limply sank, peering
    amazed—*each page was blank.*

(For oh, the supremest of our art are the stories
    we do not dare to tell,
Locked in the silence of the heart, for the awful
    records of Heav'n and Hell.)

Yet those two in the silence there seemed less
    weariful than before.
Hark! a step on the garret stair, a postman
    knocks at the flimsy door.
" Registered letter!" Brown thrills with fear;
    opens and reads, then bends above:
" Glorious tidings! Egypt, dear! The book is
    accepted—life and love!"

GOOD-BYE, LITTLE CABIN

O DEAR little cabin, I've loved you so long,
   And now I must bid you good-bye!
I've filled you with laughter, I've thrilled you
     with song,
   And sometimes I've wished I could cry.
Your walls they have witnessed a weariful fight,
   And rung to a won Waterloo:
But oh, in my triumph I'm dreary to-night—
   Good-bye, little cabin, to you!

Your roof is bewhiskered, your floor is aslant,
   Your walls seem to sag and to swing;
I'm trying to find just your faults, but I can't—
   You poor, tired, heart-broken old thing!
I've seen when you've been the best friend that I
     had,
   Your light like a gem on the snow;
You're sort of a part of me—Gee! but I'm sad;
   I hate, little cabin, to go.

GOOD-BYE, LITTLE CABIN

Below your cracked window red raspberries
    climb;
  A hornet's nest hangs from a beam;
Your rafters are scribbled with adage and
    rhyme,
  And dimmed with tobacco and dream.
"Each day has its laugh," and "Don't worry,
    just work."
  Such mottoes reproachfully shine.
Old calendars dangle—what memories lurk
  About you, dear cabin of mine!

I hear the world-call and the clang of the fight;
  I hear the hoarse cry of my kind;
Yet well do I know, as I quit you to-night,
  It's Youth that I'm leaving behind.
And often I'll think of you, empty and black,
  Moose antlers nailed over your door:
Oh, if I should perish my ghost will come back
  To dwell in you, cabin, once more!

How cold, still and lonely, how weary you seem!
  A last wistful look and I'll go.
Oh, will you remember the lad with his dream!
  The lad that you comforted so.

GOOD-BYE, LITTLE CABIN

The shadows enfold you, it's drawing to night;
  The evening star needles the sky:
And huh! but it's stinging and stabbing my
    sight—
  God bless you, old cabin, good-bye!

HEART O' THE NORTH

AND when I come to the dim trail-end,
  I who have been Life's rover,
This is all I would ask, my friend,
  Over and over and over:

A little space on a stony hill,
  With never another near me,
Sky o' the North that's vast and still,
  With a single star to cheer me;

Star that gleams on a moss-grey stone
  Graven by those who love me—
There would I lie alone, alone,
  With a single pine above me;

Pine that the north wind whinnies through—
  Oh, I have been Life's lover,
But there I'd lie and listen to
  Eternity passing over.

THE SCRIBE'S PRAYER

When from my fumbling hand the tired pen
    falls,
    And in the twilight weary droops my head;
While to my quiet heart a still voice calls,
    Calls me to join my kindred of the Dead:
Grant that I may, O Lord, ere rest be mine,
Write to Thy praise one radiant, ringing line.

For all of worth that in this clay abides,
    The leaping rapture and the ardent flame,
The hope, the high resolve, the faith that guides;
    All, all is Thine, and liveth in Thy name:
Lord, have I dallied with the sacred fire!
Lord, have I trailed Thy glory in the mire!

E'en as a toper from the dram-shop reeling,
    Sees in his garret's blackness, dazzling fair,
All that he might have been, and, heart-sick,
    kneeling,
    Sobs in the passion of a vast despair:
So my ideal self haunts me alway—
When the accounting comes, how shall I pay?

THE SCRIBE'S PRAYER

For in the dark I grope, nor understand;
  And in my heart fight selfishness and sin:
Yet, Lord, I do not seek Thy helping hand;
  Rather let me my own salvation win:
Let me through strife and penitential pain
Onward and upward to the heights attain.

Yea, let me live my life, its meaning seek;
  Bear myself fitly in the ringing fight;
Strive to be strong that I may aid the weak;
  Dare to be true—O God! the Light, the Light!
Cometh the Dark so soon?   I've mocked Thy
        word,
Yet do I know Thy Love: have mercy, Lord.

FINIS